101 QUESTIONS TO ASK BEFORE YOU GET ENGAGED

BEFORE YOU SAY 'I DO': A COMPREHENSIVE GUIDE TO EXPERT INSIGHT, ATTACHMENT STYLES, LONG-TERM RELATIONSHIPS, AND PRACTICAL GUIDANCE.

JEFFREY C. CHAPMAN

MEDIALUSION GROUP

CONTENTS

To my wife Anna,

Thank you for being my partner in crime, my partner in life, and my partner in adulting. Writing this book about 101 questions to ask before getting engaged wouldn't have been possible without your support, your encouragement, and your endless patience with my terrible puns. You truly are the glue that holds our lives together (even if that glue sometimes smells like burnt toast). So here's to us, my love, and to all the couples out there who are navigating the crazy, wonderful, and sometimes ridiculous world of adulting together. Let's raise a glass of wine (or maybe two...or three) to surviving the laundry, the bills, and the never-ending quest for the perfect avocado toast.

Cheers!

Jeff

INTRODUCTION

Engagement isn't just a shiny ring; it's a big, bright, blinking sign that says, "Fasten your seatbelt, you're about to start a lifetime journey with someone!" But wait, are you sure you have everything you need for this trip?

Welcome to a book that isn't just about love, but also about understanding, getting along, growing together, and even a little humor. It's a pre-engagement guide with 101 questions you have to answer before you say "I do." Think of this as the GPS for your relationship. It will help you find your way along the winding roads of love.

You may be wondering why these questions are so important before getting engaged. Imagine buying a car without checking the engine, the brakes, or even if it has a steering wheel. These questions are the test drive for your relationship. They lead to deep and meaningful conversations that help you learn more about your partner, yourself, and the life you want to build together.

All the questions will include all or some of the following topics:

Purpose

This part tells you why each question is important. We get to the heart of what these reveal, so you can see what's at stake.

Why it's Important

We look deeper into what these questions mean when it comes to building a strong, stable relationship that can handle life's storms.

Possible Answers

Relationships are different, and so are the answers. Explore a range of answers and think about what they mean for your journey.

Follow-up Questions

Because each answer opens up new possibilities, these are the conversations that come next, and each one is a step toward getting to know each other better.

On a Lighter Note...

Life is too short to always be serious. Some of the more serious topics will be talked about with humor, wit, and a light touch.

Positive or Negative Aspect

Nothing is either good or bad by itself. Here, we look at both sides of a situation so that you can get a full picture.

Self Reflection

Grab a mirror and look at yourself. Think about how you feel, what you've been through, and what you've learned. Use these things to create the future you want.

Practical Guidance

Advice you can use and strategies you can put into action. Advice for real-life love from the real world.

Holistic Viewpoints

Understanding love from different perspectives, such as cultural, societal, and personal ones, can help you and your partner grow closer.

For Long-term Relationships

Engagement is only the first step. Find out how to build a love that grows, develops, and lasts.

An Expert Insight

We're getting experts to help. Scholars, therapists, and relationship experts all have something to say about how to build a strong relationship.

Attachment Styles

How do you deal with these questions? Attachment theory can help you figure out this mystery and see your relationship in a new way.

So, here is your guide to exploring before getting engaged. This book is a good friend whether you're head over heels in love or still trying to figure out if you're with "The One."

Grab that ring, your partner's hand, and a sense of adventure, and let's dive in. Before you drive off into the sunset, it's time to make sure your relationship is running smoothly.

CHAPTER ONE

VALUES AND BELIEFS

UNDERSTANDING THE MORAL COMPASS THAT GUIDES US

Question #1:

What are your core values in life?

Purpose:

This question helps you figure out what your partner's morals are and how they affect their actions, decisions, and relationships. Core values are at the heart of who you are and can have a big effect on how your relationship works.

Why It's Important:

Core values deeply influence a person's decisions, actions, and life perspectives. Understanding your partner's values helps you navigate your relationship journey more harmoniously.

Possible Answers:

- "My most important values are honesty, kindness, and ambition."

- "I care most about being independent, creative, and kind.

- "My most important values are loyalty, taking care of others, and being kind."

Follow-up Questions:

- Can you give some examples of how your core values affect the things you do and the decisions you make?

- How did you come to believe what you do?

- How do your personal and professional goals match up with your values?

On a Lighter Note:

If they like being spontaneous, get ready for spontaneous weekend trips and dinner dates. You might want to keep a packed suitcase handy at all times!

Positive and Negative Aspects:

Positive: Shared values can be a strong base for a relationship that works well.

Negative: Big differences in core values can lead to views and actions that are at odds with each other, which could cause tension.

Self-Reflection:

What are your core values? Are there possible differences or similarities between your values and those of your partner? How can these be managed or utilized?

Practical Guidance:

Start by writing down what your core values are. They could be about family, honesty, having goals, being kind, doing the right thing, or other values that guide your daily lives. Share stories or examples from your own life that show how these values are put into action.

Know that you might have different values or different ways of putting things in order of importance. Explore how these differences might show up in different parts of your lives, such as career choices, relationships with friends and family, or how you spend your time and money.

Exercise: Individually write down your top five core values. Then, share them with each other and discuss why they are important to you. Consider how they influence your relationship and where there might be alignment or tension.

A Few Commonly Used Values (to get you started):

- Integrity

- Family

- Love

- Success

- Creativity

- Respect

- Wealth

- Compassion

- Responsibility

- Freedom

- Health

- Friendship

- Loyalty

- Faith

- Humility

- Knowledge

- Justice

- Courage

- Adventure

- Generosity

- Empathy

This list can help facilitate a discussion about what matters most to you and your partner. It's also worth recognizing that people may define these values differently, so exploring what each value means to both of you can be enlightening.

Holistic Viewpoints:

Core values are the foundation of what we believe and how we act. They usually come from a complex mix of things, like cultural and ethnic background, personal and family experiences, education, social influences, and personal reflections. They can include moral principles like honesty and integrity, social priorities like equality and protecting the environment, and personal goals like ambition and resiliency. People may also put different amounts of importance on their values, with some being the most important things in their lives and others being like guiding stars. Understanding this makes it easier to have conversations where everyone, no matter how different their core values are, feels heard, validated, and respected. In a world where social norms are changing and global cultures are mixing more than ever, it's important to approach this topic with a lot of sensitivity and an open mind, recognizing that people with different core values can live together peacefully and even benefit from each other.

For Long-term Relationships:

Understanding and Alignment: Since daily actions and long-term goals are based on core values, understanding and aligning them makes for a better relationship.

Ongoing Conversation: As life changes, so can values. Regular communication makes sure that both partners continue to understand and help each other as they grow.

Negotiating Differences: Having different core values doesn't have to be the end of a relationship. When people negotiate well and respect each other, it can lead to a deeper, more complex relationship.

Shared Values and Goals: Figuring out what values you and your partner have in common can help you set goals and figure out how to reach them. This strengthens the foundation of your relationship.

Question #2:

What spiritual beliefs do you have, if any?

Purpose:

This question is meant to help you learn about your partner's spiritual beliefs, or lack thereof, which can have a big effect on many parts of life and your relationship, such as how they see right and wrong, how they make decisions, and how they deal with problems.

Why It's Important:

Spiritual beliefs can affect how people live and what they think is right and wrong. The key to having a peaceful relationship is to respect each other's beliefs.

Possible Answers:

- "I call myself a [your religion] and go to church often."

- "I am an atheist and do not believe in any form of religion."

- "I think of myself as spiritual but not religious, and I meditate every day."

Follow-up Questions:

- How important is it to you that your partner believes the same things you do?

- How do your religious beliefs affect your day-to-day life and the choices you make?

- Would you be interested in learning about other ways of being spiritual?

On a Lighter Note:

If they like Zen Buddhism, you can expect a lot of meditation, quiet times, and maybe even learning how to make a zen garden. But hey, you'll always have a serene space at home!

Positive and Negative Aspects:

Positive: Shared spiritual beliefs can bring people together and help them understand each other.

Negative: Having different beliefs can lead to fights that can only be solved with respect, tolerance, and open communication.

Self-Reflection:

What are your religious or spiritual beliefs? How willing are you to learn about and respect your partner's beliefs, even if they are different from your own?

Practical Guidance:

Start by talking about your own life, how you came to believe what you do, and what that means to you. If you follow a certain religion or spiritual path, talk about its core beliefs and how they affect your daily life.

Talk about how these beliefs might affect your life together, such as how you celebrate holidays, make moral decisions, or raise your children. Find out where you might have different ideas and talk about how you can respect and honor those differences.

If spirituality is a big part of one or both of your lives, you might want to talk about how you can combine these practices or help each other with them.

Keep in mind that spiritual beliefs can change over time and that what you believe now may not be true for you in the future. By talking about this part of your relationship often, you can make sure that you both know about and support each other's spiritual journey.

Holistic Viewpoints:

Spirituality is a deeply personal journey, and people's beliefs can span a wide spectrum from traditional religious practices to atheism, agnosticism, or more modern spiritual movements. Remember that every person's spiritual path is unique and should be respected, regardless of personal beliefs.

For Long-term Relationships:

Beliefs about the spiritual world often grow and change over time, just like people do. By talking to each other often, both partners can understand how the other's spiritual journey is changing and continue to respect each other. When people have different spiritual beliefs, it can be very important to realize that they can live together peacefully. Even if the two people don't believe the same things, they can still become closer by doing spiritual activities together. If spiritual differences cause fights, having ways to disagree in a respectful way can keep the relationship strong. Also, careful planning and talking about how spiritual beliefs will affect things like raising children or celebrating holidays makes sure that everyone is on the same page and helps avoid future conflict.

Expert Insight:

Experts on relationships often say that having the same values may be more important than having the same beliefs. Even if people have different beliefs, understanding their core values can help them connect. Therapists say it's important to have empathy when dealing with different spiritual beliefs because trying to understand your partner's spiritual journey makes you feel closer to them. Some experts say that having a shared spiritual journey doesn't always mean having the same beliefs. Instead, it could mean having the same approach to exploring, growing, and helping each other on their spiritual paths. When spiritual differences cause fights, professional counseling can be a neutral place to talk about these problems with respect and understanding. Also, it's important not to make assumptions about your partner's beliefs or how they might change over time. Experts suggest asking open-ended questions and having honest conversations to encourage open communication. This shows a more nuanced understanding of how spiritual beliefs may affect long-term relationships.

Question #3:

How do you handle disagreements about your values or beliefs?

Purpose:

By asking this, you can learn how your potential partner handles arguments, especially those that involve deeply held beliefs or values. How they respond can give insight into their level of compassion, intelligence, respect, and openness to compromise.

Why It's Important:

This reveals how open-minded, respectful, and adaptable a person can be when facing ideological differences, essential for managing conflicts.

Possible Answers:

- "I try to see things from the other person's point of view and find things we agree on."

- "I stand firm because my values and beliefs are not up for discussion."

- "I try to stay out of trouble, especially when it comes to things like beliefs and values, which are sensitive."

Follow-up Questions:

- Tell me about a time when you had to handle a disagreement like that. What was the outcome?

- When reaching a compromise seems impossible, how do you proceed?

- How willing are you to change your beliefs or values if they are put into question?

On a Lighter Note:

If their idea of solving problems is to fight with lightsabers, you might want to buy a good pair of safety glasses. May the Force be with you!

Positive and Negative Aspects:

Positive: Having good skills for dealing with conflicts can help people understand each other and grow.

Negative: Being stubborn or avoiding people can make it hard to talk openly and solve problems.

Self-Reflection:

How do you deal with people who do not agree with your values or beliefs? What are some ways you can get better at handling conflicts?

Deeper Discussion:

Talk about real-life or imagined situations where people have different values or beliefs. This can help you see things from each other's points of view and understand how they make you feel.

Practical Guidance:

Before anything else, it's important to go into this conversation with a desire to understand, not to win or change. If you don't handle disagreements about values or beliefs with care and understanding, they can quickly get worse.

Start by creating a safe and respectful space where you can talk about your different points of view. Set ground rules if you need to, like don't interrupt each other, don't attack each other personally, or take a break if emotions get too high.

When talking about values or beliefs that are different from your partner's, be clear about what you believe and why, but also be willing to hear their point of view. Use "I" statements to say what you think and feel without attacking or blaming others.

Active listening means paying close attention to what your partner says without thinking of a response. Repeat what you've heard to make sure you got it right, and ask open-ended questions to learn more about their point of view.

Realize that it's okay to have different values or beliefs. The goal isn't always to come to an agreement, but to learn about each other's points of view and find ways to respect and work with those differences.

If a difference in values or beliefs affects a big decision in your relationship, you may need to find a middle ground that respects both of your points of view. This may take time, patience, and maybe even help from a professional to figure out.

Lastly, you should know that it's fine to agree to disagree. Not every argument has to be solved. The most important thing is to keep respect, empathy, and communication lines open. Bring up these conversations again if you need to, and keep working to understand and support each other, even when you disagree.

Holistic Viewpoints:

Belief systems cover a wide range and are affected by many things, such as culture, personal experiences, philosophical pondering, and spiritual exploration. They include different religious beliefs, secular humanism, agnostic skepticism, atheism, and both traditional and nontraditional spiritual practices. To keep respect and harmony in a relationship, both people must understand and accept that different belief systems are the norm, not the exception. This understanding makes it possible for people to talk to each other in a way that shows empathy and puts learning and curiosity ahead of judgment and dismissal. Each set of beliefs comes with its own set of practices, traditions, and values that can add to the richness and depth of a relationship. It is important to look at these differences with an open mind and a willingness to understand, not to convert or judge. This creates a place where people respect and admire each other, which makes room for growth and unity despite differences.

Question #4:

How do you wish to contribute positively to the world around you, and how important is it that our values align in this regard?

Purpose:

To learn how your partner sees their role in society and the world and how important shared values are to them in this context.

Why It's Important:

This question delves into the topic of personal values and aspirations, which play a critical role in shaping both individual actions and the dynamics of a relationship.

Possible Answers:

- "I believe in giving back to the community and would like to do more charity work."

- "I'm passionate about environmental issues and try to live as sustainably as possible."

- "I haven't thought much about this, but I am open to finding ways to contribute positively."

Follow-Up Questions:

- "Can you tell me more about why you care about that particular cause?"

- "How would you like us as a couple to help?"

- "Do you think that having the same values in this area is important?"

On a Lighter Note:

Imagine going out with Superman and finding out that he does not like to recycle. It is like finding out that Santa Claus is a Grinch! So, whether you are a superhero or a supervillain, it is good to know where your partner stands and if they want to save the world or just their part of the room.

Positive and Negative Aspects:

Positive: If your partner has a strong sense of social responsibility, it means they are kind, caring, and aware of how they affect the world. They probably have qualities like kindness and generosity.

Negative: On the other hand, if your partner seems uninterested or uncaring about what they can do to help the world, it could mean they do not care about other people or have a narrow view of the world. But it could also just mean that they have not thought about it much.

Self Reflection:

Think about what you value and how important it is that your partner values the same things you do. Think about how you would feel if your significant other did not share your opinion.

Practical Guidance:

When talking about this topic, it's important to make a safe, open space where both people can talk and listen without being judged. This is an investigation, not a test of compatibility, so the focus should be on genuine curiosity and understanding.

You can ask your partner questions like, "What made you feel this way?" as you share and listen to each other's thoughts. How do you think we could work together? This helps people connect and understand each other better.

At the heart of this talk is figuring out where you agree and where you might not. Alignment doesn't mean that everyone agrees on every little thing. Instead, it means that everyone supports each other's core values and big goals. You might find fun ways to work together and help each other, like volunteering together or just giving each other emotional support.

It's just as important to deal with differences with respect and grace. If there are differences, it's important to talk about how you can respect them without letting them hurt your relationship. Getting to the core values that are most important to each of you and finding areas where you agree could be helpful.

Lastly, it's good to have this conversation again now and then, keeping in mind that values and ways of contributing can change. If big disagreements turn into fights, it can be helpful to get help from a professional, like in couples counseling.

Holistic Viewpoints:

The desire to make the world a better place is a very personal thing that can show up in a lot of different ways. People can make a difference in many different ways, from helping out at a local shelter to getting ahead in a career in environmental sustainability. This desire to help is often shaped by a person's culture, socioeconomic background, and personal experiences. There is no one "right" way to interact with the world, and different points of view can even help people learn more about what it means to make a difference. It's important to go into this conversation with an open heart and mind, respecting and trying to understand how each person's unique experiences shape their view on this issue.

For Long-Term Relationships:

Long-term relationships can only work if both people share the same values and want to make the world a better place. Couples may find that their own ways of contributing change over time, or they may find new things they both like. By talking about these things often, partners can feel like they are working toward the same goals and help each other reach these goals. It's not just about finding perfect alignment, but also about seeing where there are overlaps, where compromises can be made, and where differences can be celebrated. Being open and honest about your values and what you want to accomplish can help you build a strong partnership with someone who wants to help you grow and give back.

Expert Insight:

Relationship expert, Dr. John Gottman, says in his book "The Seven Principles for Making Marriage Work"[1] that shared meaning and values are one of the most important parts of a healthy relationship. Having a common goal or similar ideas about how you want to help the world can make your connection stronger and give your relationship a solid base. It's not as important to have the same goals as it is to understand, respect, and find ways to support each other's passions and causes. Counseling or workshops for couples that focus on values can give them the tools they need to have these conversations well. Working together to make the world a better place can also give you shared experiences that make your relationship stronger and give it more meaning and fulfillment.

---

1. Gottman, J. M., & Silver, N. (2015). The Seven Principles for Making Marriage Work: A Practical Guide from the Country's Foremost Relationship Expert. Harmony. ISBN 978-0-553-41874-4.

Question #5:

How do you usually celebrate holidays?

Purpose:

This question is meant to help you learn about your partner's holiday traditions and preferences and figure out how well they might fit with your own.

Why it's Important:

During the holidays, families often get together and do things they always do. Getting to know your partner's holiday traditions can tell you a lot about what they value and how their family works. You can also think about how you might spend your holidays together.

Possible Answers:

- "I like to spend holidays with family and friends, continuing traditions from my childhood."

- "I enjoy trying new ways to celebrate holidays, like travelling or exploring different cultures."

Follow-Up Questions:

- Are there specific traditions you feel strongly about maintaining?

- How would you feel about starting new traditions together?

On a Lighter Note:

"So, do you typically spend Christmas Eve watching 'Die Hard' and arguing that it is indeed a Christmas movie? Because that's what my family does!"

Positive and Negative Aspects:

Positive: If you and your partner have similar ideas about how to celebrate holidays, it might be easier to combine your traditions.

Negative: Different holiday traditions could cause fights or disagreements, especially when it comes to choosing where and how to spend these special days.

Self-Reflection:

Think about your own holiday traditions and if you are willing to try new ones or make new ones together.

Practical Guidance:

Talk about your experiences, likes, dislikes, values, or feelings about holidays. Focusing on tradition, connection, meaning, or fun can help you figure out what shapes, supports, or challenges your celebrations.

Think about how you will handle, help each other through, or celebrate the holidays in your relationship. Think about ways to create a holiday environment that respects and combines your values, traditions, connections, and joys.

Exercise: Make a "holiday calendar" with your partner that includes both of your favorite traditions and some new ones you can do together.

Holistic Viewpoints:

Traditions from one's culture, religion, or personal life often play a role in how someone celebrates holidays. How people celebrate these special days can be deeply rooted in how they were raised and the traditions of their community. It may include unique rituals, gatherings with family and friends, special meals, or practices that honor a cultural or spiritual belief. Also, some people might choose not to celebrate certain holidays at all, or they might do things that aren't typical for those holidays. Different ways of celebrating holidays can lead to more interesting times, and learning about a partner's traditions can help a relationship grow and learn.

For Long-term Relationships:

When a couple has been together for a long time, they may find it fun to combine traditions from each of their backgrounds or make new traditions that are unique to their relationship. As a couple grows together, they may find that they come up with their own rituals that are important to them, like making a special meal, going on a trip every year, or giving back to the community. These things they do together become a part of their relationship. But it is still important for people to honor and respect each other's traditions. If people have different beliefs or ways of doing things, they may need to find a middle ground. Sharing and honoring traditions in this way helps people understand each other, deepens their emotional connections, and improves mutual respect in a relationship.

Expert Insight:

Rituals and traditions are important in relationships, and science backs this up. A study by Fiese et al.[2] that was published in the Journal of Family Psychology shows how family routines and rituals, like holiday traditions, can be helpful. Participating in these activities together has been linked to happier relationships, stronger family bonds, and a sense of identity and belonging. During times of change or stress, these rituals can become touchstones that give stability and continuity. They give people a sense of continuity and a shared history that can be passed down from one generation to the next.

---

2. Fiese, B. H., Tomcho, T. J., Douglas, M., Josephs, K., Poltrock, S., & Baker, T. (2002). A review of 50 years of research on naturally occurring family routines and rituals: Cause for celebration? Journal of Family Psychology, 16(4), 381–390.

Question #6:

What values do you want to instill in our children?

Purpose:

This question helps you figure out what your partner thinks are the most important values and lessons they want to pass on to the next generation.

Why it's Important:

Values help us decide what to do and shape how we treat other people. By teaching children the same values, you can make sure they get the same message about what is important in life.

Possible Answers:

- "Honesty, respect, kindness, and the value of hard work are some values I'd like to instill."

- "I want to instill empathy, independence, creativity, and love for learning."

Follow-Up Questions:

- How do you plan to teach these values to our children?

- How were these values instilled in you?

On a Lighter Note:

"Remember, it's not only about teaching them to say 'please' and 'thank you.' It's also about teaching them how to use a smartphone better than us!"

Positive and Negative Aspects:

Positive: You learn more about your partner's values and what they want their children to learn.

Negative: If your partner's values are different from yours, you might not agree with each other.

Self-Reflection:

What are the values that are non-negotiable for you? What did your parents teach you that you would like to teach others?

Practical Guidance:

To figure out how to raise children together, it's important to know what values you both hold.

Talk about how you feel, what you want, or what you value about teaching children values, such as ethics, character, empathy, resilience, or social responsibility. Focus on personal beliefs, cultural influences, or societal expectations to find out what these values have in common with, what drives them, or what shapes them.

Find out how you and your partner will teach or instill these values in your children. This will help you and your partner have a shared understanding, be consistent, set good examples, or get on the same page.

Exercise: Make a document together called "family values" that lists the rules you both agree to teach your children.

Holistic Viewpoints:

Many different things influence the values that parents want to teach their children:

Different cultures stress different things, like individualism, community, honor, family ties, and so on. Recognizing and respecting these differences can help the children build a strong set of morals.

Religious Beliefs: If one or both partners have a certain religious belief, it can affect the values they want to teach their children, such as kindness, faith, honesty, etc.

Personal Experiences: The values that parents think are important may also be shaped by their own life experiences, education, and personal philosophies.

For Long-term Relationships:

Couples who have been together for a long time may have already set some family values. Still, this is a process that is always changing:

Reflecting on Current Values: Take stock of the values that are already being taught and think about how well they work and if they are still important as the family changes.

Adding New Values: As the kids get older or the family faces new problems, new values may become important.

Making sure there is consistency: Both partners should agree on the core values and make sure they are taught and shown in the same way.

CHAPTER TWO

PERSONAL GOALS AND FUTURE PLANS

ENVISIONING A FUTURE TOGETHER

Question #7:

What are your life goals, and how do you plan to achieve them?

Purpose:

Your partner's answers to this question will give you insight into their goals, aspirations, and overall life plan. Learning about one another's aspirations is essential for figuring out how well they mesh with your own and how you can help each other succeed.

Why It's Important:

This question gives insight into a person's ambitions, motivations, and their approach to life planning. It helps understand if the couple's future paths align or can be harmonized.

Possible Answers:

Answers could range from starting a business to climbing Mount Everest to writing a novel. Each response reveals something about their doggedness, ingenuity, and dedication.

Follow-up Questions:

- How have your goals changed as you have gone through life?

- What do you see as potential roadblocks to your success, and how would you plan to overcome them?

- How can I support you in reaching these goals?

On a Lighter Note:

If your significant other has dreams of starting a Martian colony, you should probably get some zero-gravity training. And if they're aiming for the Nobel Peace Prize, I hope you're good with sharing the spotlight at gala dinners!

Positive and Negative Aspects:

Positive: Having similar life goals can result in a synergistic relationship in which both partners grow together.

Negative: Divergent goals, on the other hand, may cause friction if not properly communicated and negotiated.

Self-Reflection:

Consider your own life objectives. Are they compatible with those of your partner? If not, where can you find common ground? How willing are you to help each other?

Practical Guidance:

In a long-term relationship, it's important to understand and share the same life goals. Think about the following steps to deal with this:

Find Your Individual Goals: To start, make a separate list of your short-term and long-term life goals. Think about your career, your family, your personal growth, and your free time.

Share and Discuss: Tell each other your goals and why they're important to you. Look for areas where you agree and where you disagree.

Find Possible Conflicts: Look for any goals that might be at odds with each other. For example, if one partner wants to move around a lot for work but the other wants to stay put at home, that's an area that needs work.

Make goals that you and your partner can both work toward. This will help you find common ground. This could mean finding a balance between traveling and staying in one place or agreeing on plans for money or the family.

Make a Roadmap: List the steps you can take to reach these goals. Set deadlines, give out tasks, and plan regular check-ins to see how things are going.

Keep the lines of communication open: As you work toward your goals, make sure there is constant conversation. Life goals can change, and constant communication makes it possible to make changes and realign.

If you need to, get professional help to make sure your goals are aligned. Don't be afraid to get help from a professional, like couples counseling, to make these conversations easier.

Celebrate Successes: When you reach important goals, make a big deal out of it. Appreciating each other's work makes the relationship stronger.

Holistic Viewpoints:

Life goals are very personal and depend on a lot of different things. Recognizing these things can help the relationship grow in empathy and understanding:

Sociocultural background: Different cultures, societies, and communities often place different values and rules at the center of their lives, which can affect how people choose to live their lives. For a kind conversation about goals, it's important to understand and respect these differences.

Personal Experiences and Early Life: A person's life goals are shaped by their past experiences, education, and early life. Knowing your partner's story can help you understand their goals and why they want to reach them better.

Changing Life Circumstances: When things in our lives change, like getting a new job, becoming a parent, or growing as a person, our goals may also change. Recognizing that life goals change over time makes it clear that aligning them is not a one-time conversation but an ongoing one.

Intersections with Other Parts of Life: Life goals are often connected to other important parts of life, such as planning for money, health, spiritual beliefs, and family relationships. Seeing how these things are connected makes it possible to talk about them in a more complete and nuanced way.

Possible Conflicts and Compromises: If people have different life goals, there may be problems. Getting through these problems can be easier if people work together, accept each other's differences, and look for things they have in common.

The Importance of Flexibility: Putting an emphasis on being flexible when setting and pursuing life goals can help people get along better. Partners can support each other's individual goals while working toward shared goals when there is flexibility.

Inclusion of Both Partners' Voices: Making sure that both partners are actively involved in defining and supporting each other's goals promotes a balanced and fair relationship.

Think about the timing: Some life goals may not be possible right away or may need to be put in a different order. A holistic view takes into account the timing and order of goals in relation to life stages or other important things.

For Long-term Relationships:

Talking about life goals is not a one-time thing. People keep talking about it because their goals change over time. In a long-term relationship, you should discuss this topic often to keep each other's support and understanding.

Expert Insight:

Sharing goals with similar others intensifies goal pursuit, resulting in more goal-congruent behavior, as demonstrated in two experiments where participants produced greater promotion or prevention behaviors when their goals were shared with similar others compared to different others.[1]

---

1. Garriy Shteynberg and A. Galinsky. "Implicit coordination: Sharing goals with similar others intensifies goal pursuit." Journal of Experimental Social Psychology, 47 (2011): 1291-1294.

Question #8:

Where do you see yourself in five years?

Purpose:

The answer to this question can tell you a lot about how your partner sees the future, how ambitious they are, and what they want to do with their lives. It can show you if your ideas about the future match up with theirs.

Why It's Important:

It's important to know if a partner's short-term goals are the same as or similar to your own. This way, expectations can be set and plans can be made together.

Possible Answers:

- "I see myself advancing in my career and possibly in a leadership role."

- "I'd love to be exploring new cultures around the world."

- "I see myself running my own successful business."

- "I'd like to settle down and start a family with you."

Follow-up Questions:

- How flexible is this vision for the future?

- What steps are you taking to actualize these plans?

- How do I feature in your future plans?

On a Lighter Note:

If they picture themselves lounging on a Bali beach while you picture yourself navigating the wilds of Alaska, it may be time to come to an accommodation. A tropical cabin in Hawaii, anyone?

Positive and Negative Aspects:

Positive: Aligned future visions can provide a clear direction for your relationship.

Negative: Vastly different visions can cause tension if not addressed proactively and sensitively.

Self-Reflection:

Take some time to think about your own vision for the next five years. How does it complement or contrast with the goals that your partner has set? Are you willing to make concessions if they turn out to be necessary?

Practical Guidance:

The question "Where do you see yourself in five years?" is more than just a way to start a casual conversation. It shows what your hopes, goals, and plans are for your life. It includes professional growth, personal growth, the dynamics of relationships, and even preferences about where to live. But how do you approach a question that seems simple but is actually very deep in a way that is thoughtful, strategic, and good for your relationship?

Start by both writing down your personal and professional goals for the next five years. This could include goals for a career, education, starting a family, or traveling. Take the time to talk about these goals in an open and honest way, and don't be afraid to get into the details.

Next, look at how each partner's vision fits with or differs from that of the other. This evaluation helps you figure out where you might get along and where you might not. Here, you can start to see how your paths might connect or split.

From there, you can come up with a plan that fits both of your goals. This process of working together not only builds a sense of unity but also makes it possible for people to help and support each other.

But that's not the end of the work. The creation of this shared vision leads to the setting of milestones that can be reached, the allocation of resources, and the determination of how much help each partner needs to give. This step helps turn vague ideas into plans that can be carried out.

It's just as important to think about possible problems and talk about how to deal with them. By preparing for these possible problems ahead of time, you'll be able to handle them with grace and strength.

Regular check-ins can make sure that your five-year plan is still in line with your changing needs, wants, and circumstances. These talks show how important it is for a relationship to have open communication and be flexible.

Last, be happy about how far you've come. Recognizing accomplishments, no matter how big or small, helps people feel good about working together.

Holistic Viewpoints:

The answer to the question "Where do you see yourself in five years?" reveals a lot about a person's personality, goals, lifestyle choices, and even fears or doubts. Some people might have a very clear and detailed plan for their future, based on their career or personal goals. Others might be more spontaneous and value being flexible and open to opportunities that come up out of the blue. Both of these points of view are true, but they come from different ideas about life, success, happiness, and control. Understanding and appreciating where your partner is coming from in this situation can help both of you feel more empathy and respect for each other.

For Long-term Relationships:

People's hopes and goals change as their lives do. Whether it's because of a change in career path, planning for a family, health issues, or personal growth, the answer to this question could change a lot over time. By having this conversation again and again, both partners can make sure they are still on the same page and can still support each other's changing goals and dreams.

Expert Insight:

Both career coaches and relationship experts stress how important it is for long-term goals to be in sync. Even though it's not necessary for both partners to have the same plans for the next five years, knowing each other's plans can help build support, reduce fights, and help plan joint projects like buying a house or growing the family. It's not just about the goals themselves, but also about how those goals show what you value, what you want, and what you expect. When you recognize and talk about these deeper issues, this seemingly simple question can be a powerful way to deepen your connection and work together in a relationship.

Question #9:

What are your retirement plans?

Purpose:

This question tells you about your partner's long-term goals, how they plan for their finances, and how they feel about work-life balance. A person's retirement plan can tell a lot about what is important to them and what they value.

Why It's Important:

Retirement plans reflect a person's long-term goals and lifestyle preferences. Discussing this early on ensures both parties can plan their future accordingly.

Possible Answers:

- "I plan to retire early and travel the world."

- "I want to move to the country and live a quiet life there."

- "I don't see myself fully retiring; I'd like to keep working on passion projects."

Follow-up Questions:

- How are you preparing financially for your retirement?

- How does work fit into your life post-retirement?

- How do our retirement plans align or differ?

On a Lighter Note:

If they want to retire on a remote island, they might need to get used to drinking coconut water and spearfishing. On the bright side, you can finally get the beach body you have always wanted: a body... on a beach.

Positive and Negative Aspects:

Positive: A shared vision of retirement can be a good thing because it gives both a goal to work toward.

Negative: On the other hand, having different plans for retirement may require compromise and negotiation.

Self-Reflection:

Think about what you want out of retirement. How does it fit with the vision of your partner? What kinds of compromises or ways of working together can you think of? Retirement is not just about quitting your job; it is also about how you want to spend your later years. To get through this phase together, you need to talk about your lifestyle, where you want to live, what you want to do, and your financial plans.

Practical Guidance:

Start by envisioning what retirement looks like for both of you. This might include things like travel, hobbies, volunteering, or spending more time with family and friends. Understand that each person's vision might be different, so finding common ground and compromise will be crucial.

Next, take the time to carefully consider your financial needs. Talk openly about your expectations for your standard of living, your current savings, and the steps you both might need to take to reach your goals. Consulting a financial planner who specializes in retirement can be a wise move here to align your visions with your actual financial situation.

Your health and wellness should also be part of this conversation. This includes planning for potential healthcare needs, insurance considerations, and even living arrangements if mobility becomes an issue. These decisions can significantly impact both your lifestyle and finances.

Discuss the location and living arrangements. Whether you want to downsize, move closer to family, or even live part of the year in a different climate, these decisions should reflect your shared vision and financial planning.

Recognize that retirement planning is an ongoing process. Your plans might change as your life changes, so keep the lines of communication open. Regularly revisit and revise your plans, if necessary, to ensure they continue to align with your evolving needs and desires.

Holistic Viewpoints:

Retirement plans are very personal and have many different parts. They include financial security, health care needs, lifestyle choices, family concerns, and even career choices after retirement. Some people may have clear goals that include travel, hobbies, or helping the community, while others may have more open or changing plans. Realizing that these plans are often complicated and show a person's whole life journey can help people talk to each other in a more understanding and thorough way.

For Long-term Relationships:

Talking about retirement is not a one-time thing. As both people age and change, their ideas about retirement may also change. This could mean putting health, family, location, leisure activities, or even going back to work in a different role as a priority. By keeping the lines of communication open and being flexible about these changes, both partners' needs and wishes can be met, leading to a more fulfilling and happy retirement life together.

Expert Insight:

Financial planners and relationship therapists stress how important it is to talk openly and early about retirement goals and the steps that need to be taken to reach them. Couples can avoid misunderstandings and fights in the future if they take each partner's wants and expectations into account and work together to create a shared vision. Whether it's coming up with a plan for money together or deciding where to live, these talks set the stage for a successful and happy retirement. Cooperative planning and regular check-ins can help bring these different ideas into line, fostering harmony and mutual support as a couple approaches this big change.

CHAPTER THREE

CAREER AND WORK

BALANCING PROFESSIONAL AMBITIONS AND PERSONAL LIVES

Question #10:

Do you plan to have a career change in the future?

Purpose:

This question reveals your partner's job satisfaction, career goals, and willingness to change. A potential career change could have a significant impact on aspects such as income, lifestyle, and location.

Why It's Important:

Changes in careers can have a big effect on a couple's way of life, finances, and time together. The open talk will help you get ready for these kinds of changes.

Possible Answers:

- "I am satisfied with my current career path."

- "I've been thinking about shifting to a different industry."

- "One day, I hope to start my own business."

Follow-up Questions:

- What is making you want to switch careers?

- How could a possible change in careers affect our plans for the future?

- How can I help you through this change?

On a Lighter Note:

If your partner is thinking about transitioning from a corporate job to a career as a mime artist, you should start practicing your miming skills. On the bright side, arguments will be quieter!

Positive and Negative Aspects:

Positive: A career change may result in a happier, more satisfied partner.

Negative: It may cause uncertainty, financial fluctuations, and significant adjustments.

Self-Reflection:

Consider how your partner's potential career change may affect your shared future. Are you prepared to help them through this transition?

Practical Guidance:

To answer this question, you need to not only think about it on your own but also carefully talk with your partner and plan together.

Start by trying to figure out why you might want to change careers. Are you looking for more happiness, financial security, or a better balance between work and life? If you know the "why" behind this decision, you can take a more careful and well-thought-out approach.

Talk about what a change in career could mean for the relationship. This could include things like money, changing work hours, moving, or the possible need for more schooling or training. By talking openly about these possible effects, you can avoid misunderstandings and create a supportive environment.

Make a plan with your partner that shows how you can help each other through this possible change. This plan could include setting financial goals, making a timeline for the career change, and figuring out how the other partner can help and encourage.

Think about possible problems that could come up and talk about how to solve them. When you change jobs, there are often a lot of unknowns and challenges. Getting ahead of these problems can help you deal with them with confidence and strength.

Lastly, make a plan for how often you will talk about this again. Changing careers is often a decision that needs to be talked about and changed over time. Regular check-ins can help make sure that both partners are still on the same page and supporting each other, even if their goals and circumstances change.

Holistic Viewpoints:

The way someone feels about changing careers shows more than just their personal tastes; it shows how they see life and how they want to grow as a person. Some people may want to keep growing and learning in their careers, while others may want to be stable and stay in the same field for a long time. To understand each other's views on changing careers, you have to look into what you think about taking risks, being successful, failing, and what makes a happy life.

For Long-term Relationships:

In a long-term relationship, career plans and goals are not set in stone; they can change as people grow, find new passions, or face opportunities or challenges they didn't expect. To keep both partners on the same page, it's important to talk about future career changes in an open and honest way. It helps people help each other, understand what they might have to give up or change, and create a shared vision of the future.

Question #11:

Would you be willing to relocate for work or any other reason?

Purpose:

This question is about how flexible and open to change you are, especially when it comes to geography. It is essential to know if one person is attached to a particular place and the other is willing to try new things.

Why It's Important:

Relocation could mean leaving behind family, friends, and familiar environments. Understanding each other's willingness to relocate can prevent potential disagreements in the future.

Possible Answers:

- "Yes, I'd love to live in different places around the world."

- "I might, but only if I never get the chance again."

- "No, I'd rather stay close to where I came from and my family."

Follow-up Questions:

- What would make you think about moving somewhere else?

- Which places or countries do you most want to visit?

- How would us moving away change the way we feel about each other?

On a Lighter Note:

If your partner wants to live in the Swiss Alps but you can not imagine living anywhere but on the beach, you might want to look into coastal cities that also have skiing. San Diego, anyone?

Positive and Negative Aspects:

Positive: Being open to moving together can lead to new and exciting adventures and life experiences.

Negative: On the other hand, if one person is more set in their ways, it could lead to hard choices and possible compromise.

Self-Reflection:

Think about whether or not you are willing to move. How do your partner's views align with yours? Are you prepared for a potential compromise?

Practical Guidance:

Moving for work or any other reason is a big choice that affects many parts of your life, including your relationships. When asked this question, it's important to first understand the reasoning behind it. Do you want to move because of a job, your family, or your own need for change? If you know the "why," you can steer the whole conversation.

Next, you and your partner should work together to figure out what will happen. How would moving affect your jobs, relationships with family and friends, and way of life? It's not just the person who wants to move who needs to think about how it will affect their life and their goals as a couple.

Exploring different options can help you be flexible and find a middle ground. Maybe a temporary long-distance arrangement could work, or maybe you could both be happier in a different place. To find solutions, it's important to keep an open mind and work together.

Making a plan for the move together is also very important. This plan will tell you how to do everything, from looking into new places to live to figuring out how to move. Working together makes sure that both partners are on board with the plan and know what to expect.

The dynamics of the relationships should also be thought about. How will you both get used to meeting new people and doing things differently? You can get through these changes together if you talk to each other in an open and honest way.

Lastly, you might want to think about building a support system in your new place. How will you make new connections if you move away from people you know? And keep in mind that, like many important life choices, the decision to move may change over time. Regular check-ins make sure that everyone is still on the same page and helping each other.

Holistic Viewpoints:

Being willing to move is often about a lot more than just a career choice. It talks about deep-seated values, personal priorities, ties to community and family, preferences in lifestyle, and individual goals. Some people like to move to new places because they are exciting and offer new opportunities, while others feel very connected to where they are now. When making this choice, it's important to think about a partner's needs, goals, ties to family and community, and whether they want to live in the city or the country.

For Long-term Relationships:

The question of moving is rarely brought up just once. This is especially true in today's fast-paced, globalized world. It may need to be looked at again at different times, like when you're thinking about a new job, growing your family, taking care of aging parents, or making other changes to your life. The key to making a supportive environment is to talk about feelings, fears, and goals in a way that is open and honest. It also lets people come up with a shared vision or, if necessary, make a plan for what to do if something goes wrong.

Question #12:

Do you want to start a business of your own?

Purpose:

This question uncovers your partner's entrepreneurial spirit, risk tolerance, and aspirations. This is important to know because starting a business can have big effects on your time, money, and way of life.

Why It's Important:

Starting a business often requires a substantial investment of time, energy, and finances. Discussing this will set clear expectations about future commitments.

Possible Answers:

- "Yes, I've always dreamed of running my own company."

- "Maybe, if I have a viable idea and resources."

- "No, I prefer the stability of traditional employment."

Follow-up Questions:

- What kind of business would you like to start?

- How would this affect our shared lifestyle and finances?

- How can I support you in this endeavor?

On a Lighter Note:

If your business idea with your partner is to raise exotic snails for high-end restaurants, you might need to learn to like escargot. On the plus side, you will have a lot of slow-moving pets!

Positive and Negative Aspects:

Positive: A successful business can give you freedom and money.

Negative: On the other hand, it is often risky, can be hard on your finances, and takes a lot of time away from the relationship.

Self-Reflection:

Think about how comfortable you are with the risks and rewards of starting your own business. Can you give your partner the support and understanding they need if they choose this path? Starting a business is a big decision that can affect a couple's lifestyle, finances, and time management in a lot of ways. Having a detailed discussion about these factors is crucial.

Practical Guidance:

Find out why you want to start a business in the first place. Is it about achieving a long-held goal, becoming financially independent, or following a unique idea? Understanding the "why" will help you see things more clearly and set the tone for future talks.

Next, think about how to start a business in the real world. This means learning about the industry, making a business plan, figuring out how much money you need, and figuring out what risks and rewards you might face. By researching and talking about these things together, you can get a better idea of what it takes to start a business.

Talk about how this business would affect your relationship and how you live your life. Will they have to spend more time apart? How will risks to money be handled? Addressing these worries right away can help prevent misunderstandings in the future.

If you need to, think about getting help from a professional. Talking to a financial advisor, business mentor, or other professional can give you valuable, situation-specific advice.

Check to see how this decision fits with other goals and values that everyone shares. How does the fact that one partner is starting a business fit with the career or personal goals of the other partner? Finding alignment makes sure that the business adds to the relationship and doesn't hurt it.

Holistic Viewpoints:

People often want to start their own business because of their values, upbringing, passions, personalities, and even cultural expectations. Some people may want to be on their own, be creative, be in charge, make money, or make a difference in society. Some people may like the security, structure, and stability that come with working for a well-known company. Understanding the fears, hopes, and fears that led to this decision can tell you a lot about a person's character, priorities, and way of life.

For Long-Term Relationships:

The decision to start a business doesn't just affect the person who wants to do it; it affects both partners in a relationship. Because of this, it needs to keep talking and be flexible. Because of the way entrepreneurship works, business plans and directions can change and change quickly. So, an ongoing conversation in which both partners talk about their feelings, expectations, and roles can help build a relationship that is both supportive and flexible. It lets people plan their lives together, including money, time, responsibilities, and even risk management, all of which can change over time as business life goes up and down.

Expert Insight:

Entrepreneurship is often seen as a romantic idea, but in reality, it can be stressful, full of uncertainty, take a lot of time, and be hard on your finances, especially in the beginning. Experts on relationships and studies that look at entrepreneurial couples point out the importance of strong and open communication, making decisions together, and setting clear boundaries. For these problems to be solved, people usually need to agree on what they will have to give up and what they will get out of it, and they also need to be prepared to deal with possible stresses and strains. Experts say that respect, empathy, and support for each other, as well as a willingness to change and renegotiate roles and responsibilities, can help couples turn the challenges of being an entrepreneur into chances to grow as a couple and get closer.

Question #13:

How do you balance work and personal life?

Purpose:

To figure out how your partner feels about work-life balance and how they handle their professional and personal obligations.

Why it's Important:

By looking at how a person balances their work and personal life, you can learn about their priorities, how they use their time, and how they might handle shared responsibilities in the future.

Possible Answers:

- "I try to stick to regular working hours and reserve weekends for relaxation and personal activities."

- "I often have to work late, but I always make sure to dedicate quality time to my personal life and relationships."

Follow-Up Questions:

- How do you handle stress from work without letting it affect our relationship?

- What activities help you disconnect from work and focus on personal life?

On a Lighter Note:

"Balancing work and personal life is like a yoga pose – it requires flexibility, focus, and the occasional wobble is absolutely fine!"

Positive and Negative Aspects:

Positive: Having a good work-life balance shows that you can manage your time well, deal with stress in a healthy way, and care about your own health and relationships.

Negative: If a person has trouble balancing work and life, it could cause problems and make them unhappy in the future. They might put work ahead of their own time or vice versa.

Self-Reflection:

Think about how you balance work and life. Do you feel like you have a good balance? What can you learn from the way your partner does things, and what can they teach you?

Practical Guidance:

Talk about your experiences, problems, or ways to keep your work and personal life in balance. Focusing on your values, needs, commitments, or well-being can help you figure out what helps or hurts your balance.

Find out how you and your partner will handle, help each other with, or balance work and personal life. Think about how you can create an environment that supports your values, needs, way of life, and well-being. What might be involved in terms of mutual understanding, flexibility, working together, or planning together?

Exercise: Set up regular "check-in" times to talk about how both partners feel about the balance. Think about having "unplugged" times when everyone stops working to spend time with each other.

Holistic Viewpoints:

Work-life balance looks very different in different cultures, jobs, personal situations, and stages of a career. For example, a person with a demanding or high-pressure job might find it hard to keep their balance, especially when they are working on a very important project. On the other hand, someone with a more flexible job or who is further along in their career may have more control over their work-life balance. How people see and deal with this balance also depends on their own preferences, the needs of their families, and their overall way of life. Work-life balance is not a one-size-fits-all idea, and what works for one person might not work for another. Because of this, empathy and understanding are very important when talking about this topic, especially when it comes to relationships.

For Long-term Relationships:

In long-term relationships, a healthy work-life balance requires constant communication and the ability to change. As work demands, personal needs, family responsibilities, and other aspects of life change over time, so must the way partners find this balance. Regular talks about how each person feels about the current balance and what changes might be needed can help each person understand and support the other. This ongoing negotiation helps make sure that both partners' needs are met, which is good for the health and resilience of the relationship as a whole. Long-term relationships need trust, openness, and a willingness to put each other's happiness first in order to have a good work-life balance.

Expert Insight:

Researchers have learned a lot about how work-life balance, job satisfaction, and overall life satisfaction are linked. According to the study by Kossek and Ozeki[1], having a good balance between work and personal life is a big part of being happy in general. This affects more than just an individual's happiness; it also changes the way relationships and families work.

Organizations also know how important it is to have a good balance between work and life, and many have policies in place to help employees deal with these different demands. People think that encouraging a good balance between work and life is not only the right thing to do but also a way to boost productivity and keep employees. Realizing that a

---

1. Kossek, E., & Ozeki, C. (1998). Work-family conflict, policies, and the
   job-life satisfaction relationship: A review and directions for organizational
   behavior-human resources research. Journal of Applied Psychology, 83(2),
   139–149.

person who is happy in both their personal and professional lives is more likely to be happy and engaged is a powerful realization for both employers and employees.

Question #14:

Are you okay with me working late or on weekends if necessary?

Purpose:

The goal of this question is to find out how understanding and flexible your partner is when it comes to work obligations that may cut into personal time.

Why it's Important:

Work responsibilities can sometimes take up more time, which can mess up personal plans. Having a partner who understands and supports these necessary responsibilities can reduce stress and the chance of arguments.

Possible Answers:

"I understand that sometimes work demands extra hours, as long as it doesn't become the norm and infringe on our personal time."

"I'd prefer if we could keep work and personal life separate, but I know it's not always possible and would support you when necessary."

Follow-Up Questions:

How would we ensure that our relationship does not suffer because of work commitments?

How would you handle feelings of neglect if I needed to work extended hours for a period of time?

On a Lighter Note:

"If working late means you'll occasionally bring home takeout, then count me in! Just kidding, I understand that work sometimes requires us to put in extra hours."

Positive and Negative Aspects:

Positive: Being flexible and understanding about a partner's work schedule can lead to mutual respect and a supportive environment.

Negative: If a partner has strict rules about how much time they want to spend together, it could make things difficult when work needs extra hours.

Self-Reflection:

Think about how flexible you are and what you would do if your partner had to work late or on the weekend.

Practical Guidance:

Talk about how you feel, what you need, what you value, or what worries you about working late or on weekends. Focusing on your lifestyle, commitments, well-being, or trust can help you figure out what might help or hinder you in dealing with this part of your work-life.

Find out how you will handle, help, or adjust to your partner working late or on the weekends. Think about ways to help people understand each other, be flexible, build trust, or talk about their work schedules and other commitments.

Exercise: Write a "work agreement" that spells out expectations, how you want to communicate, and how special events will be handled to keep the relationship healthy.

Holistic Viewpoints:

Different relationships feel differently about whether or not it's okay for a partner to work late or on the weekends. It could be very helpful for people who work in jobs with a lot of stress, have irregular hours, or have more than one job. When family responsibilities, personal needs, and expectations from a relationship come into play, the situation gets more complicated. The answer to this question can be very different depending on who is being asked, what their values are, and what their life is like. What's okay in one relationship could be a source of conflict in another. So, to answer this question, you need to know about both partners' work situations, expectations for the relationship, and personal values.

For Long-term Relationships:

When two people are together for a long time, their work schedules and obligations may change and sometimes get harder. As people move up in their careers, there may be more opportunities or higher expectations that require them to work longer hours. These changes can have an effect on the relationship, so it's important to talk openly and often about how work obligations fit with relationship goals and family needs. Couples can get through these problems without putting their relationship at risk by being flexible, understanding, and reevaluating their relationship often. This constant communication builds trust and makes sure that both partners have the same ideas about how to balance their work and personal lives. This makes it less likely that there will be disagreements or misunderstandings.

Expert Insight:

Research backs up the idea that knowing and working around a partner's busy work schedule, even if it's hard, makes the relationship happier. A study by Wight, Raley, and Bianchi in the Journal of Marriage and Family[2] points out how important support and empathy are in this situation.

The study shows that support and understanding are more important than the amount of time spent together. What really matters is whether or not partners are willing to respect each other's professional responsibilities and work hard to stay close and connected. Stress

---

2. Wight, V. R., Raley, S. B., & Bianchi, S. M. (2008). Time for children, one's spouse and oneself among parents who work nonstandard hours. Social Forces, 87(1), 243–271.

caused by busy work schedules can be lessened by doing things like setting aside time for quality time and talking openly about feelings and expectations.

Question #15:

How ambitious are you in your career?

Purpose:

This question is meant to help you figure out your partner's career goals, what drives them, and how they plan to reach their goals.

Why it's Important:

When you know what your partner wants to do with their career, you can learn about their work ethic, values, and expectations about work-life balance. It can also change how you decide to move, plan your finances, or even start a family.

Possible Answers:

- "I'm highly ambitious and constantly strive for growth and better positions in my career."

- "I'm content as long as I'm able to do what I love and maintain a work-life balance."

Follow-Up Questions:

- What's your ultimate career goal?

- How do you plan to achieve your career goals?

On a Lighter Note:

"As long as your career ambition doesn't involve becoming a professional couch potato, we're good!"

Positive and Negative Aspects:

Positive: Understanding your partner's goals can help you be ready to make sacrifices, like working long hours or going on a lot of trips.

Negative: Conflicts can happen when one partner's goals require big sacrifices from the other or when their goals are very different.

Self-Reflection:

How do your career goals and those of your partner match up? What are you willing to give up to help your partner get ahead in their career?

Practical Guidance:

In a career, ambition can take many forms, and it's important to know what drives you and your partner. When someone is ambitious, they might want to get a promotion, find creative fulfillment, or start their own business.

Talk about where you want to be in your career in the future and what you are willing to give up to get there. If both partners understand these things, they can help each other reach their career goals.

Exercise: Make career vision boards on your own and show them to each other. Talk about how these ideas fit together or don't, and what compromises or help might be needed to make these dreams come true.

Holistic Viewpoints:

Career ambition is a very personal thing that can vary a lot from person to person:

Different cultures may put different amounts of importance on career success. In some cultures, it may be important to be ambitious about your career, while in others, it may be more important to be involved with your family or community.

Gender Expectations: Gender roles in society can affect how people see and pursue their career goals. It is important to understand these ideas and try to change them.

Personal values and interests: For some, moving up in their careers may be the most important thing, while for others, personal growth, family, hobbies, or other interests may be more important.

For Long-term Relationships:

Both people's career goals may change over the course of a long-term relationship, depending on things like family, health, or personal growth:

Open Communication: Talking about career goals together on a regular basis makes sure that both people are on the same page and can support each other's goals.

Needs and Goals: In long-term relationships, it's important to find a balance between career goals, family needs, relationship goals, and your own well-being. It may be necessary to negotiate and find a middle ground.

Understanding Changes: A person's career goals may change over time due to changes in the job market, personal interests, family needs, and other things. Accepting these changes and making adjustments together can make the relationship stronger.

Question #16:

Would you support me if my career required a lot of traveling?

Purpose:

The point of this question is to see how flexible and willing your partner is to adapt to changes or demands in your career, especially if it involves a lot of travel.

Why it's Important:

The answer to this question can tell you what your partner wants from the time you spend together, how flexible they are, and if they are willing to support your career even if it means you spend less time together physically.

Possible Answers:

- "Yes, I understand that careers sometimes require sacrifices, and I would be supportive."

- "It would be hard, but we can make it work with good communication and planning."

Follow-Up Questions:

- How would we maintain our connection if I had to be away for extended periods of time?

- What are your concerns about having a partner who travels frequently for work?

On a Lighter Note:

"I'll support you...and your airline miles. Does this mean we're finally going on that trip to the Maldives?"

Positive and Negative Aspects:

Positive: This conversation can help you plan for a career-related trip in the future and set expectations about how you will talk and spend time together.

Negative: If your partner does not like the idea of you traveling a lot for work, it could put stress on your relationship and force you to talk more and make concessions.

Self-Reflection:

Think about whether you are willing to make changes and sacrifices in your relationship to meet the needs of your or your partner's career.

Practical Guidance:

A relationship can be affected in many ways by the needs of a job that requires a lot of travel.

Talk about the type and frequency of the travel, how it might affect your time together, and how you'll stay in touch while you're away. Talk about any worries you have or hopes you have.

Exercise: Make a "travel agreement" that says how you'll stay in touch, share responsibilities, and be there for each other emotionally. Review this agreement often and make changes as needed.

Holistic Viewpoints:

Different people and cultures have different ideas about what it means to travel for work:

Personal and cultural context: Traveling for work is seen as a sign of success or dedication in some cultures or professions. In other places, it might be seen as a sacrifice that needs to be made or even as a disruption to family life.

Personal Preferences: Some people might love the chance to travel because they see it as a chance to try new things or grow as a person. Others might see it as a challenge, especially if they have strong ties to their local community, family obligations, or health concerns.

Compatibility with Life Stage: Traveling may be easier to handle at some stages of life and harder at others, such as when you have young children or are taking care of aging parents.

For Long-term Relationships:

Regular travel can present long-term relationships with both challenges and opportunities:

Open Communication: It's important for couples to talk about and re-negotiate their terms as their jobs change. This can mean talking about feelings, setting limits, and finding ways to stay connected even though you live far away.

Trust and Independence: Frequent travel might require both partners to have a lot of trust in each other and to be able to keep some independence.

Making decisions together: When making big decisions, like taking a job that requires a lot of travel, both partners should be involved. Some things to think about are the benefits of the job, how long it is expected to take to travel, and how it might affect the relationship and family life.

Expert Insight:

Having a relationship and a busy career, especially one that requires travel, takes conscious effort:

Relationship upkeep: Relationships need to be cared for. Even when you're far away, technologies like video calls can help you stay close.

Support Systems: Whether it's friends, family, or the community, a strong support system can be very helpful, especially for the partner who stays at home.

Quality over quantity: It's not always about how much time you spend with someone, but how well you spend that time. Prioritizing meaningful, high-quality time together can make up for long periods of being apart.

How to Figure Out the Trade-Offs: There are pros and cons to every job choice. When both partners understand the pros and cons of frequent travel, they can make better decisions and help each other.

CHAPTER FOUR

COMMITMENT AND MARRIAGE

EXPLORING THE BOND THAT UNITES US

Question #17:

What does commitment mean to you?

Purpose:

To find out what your partner knows and thinks about commitment. Does it mean that they have the same Netflix account or that they have the same tattoos?

Why It's Important:

Understanding each other's views on commitment can set the foundation for relationship expectations and boundaries.

Possible Answers:

- "To be committed means to stick together through good times and bad. It is a promise to help and support each other."

- "To me, commitment means putting time and effort into a relationship and trusting each other."

Follow-up Questions:

- How would you express your commitment to your partner?

- What does a lack of commitment look like to you?

On a Lighter Note:

If they say, "Commitment is knowing your partner's favorite pizza topping," you might be dealing with a culinary Romeo. But hey, there are worse things than a lifetime of perfectly ordered pizza!

Positive and Negative Aspects:

Positive: A strong relationship can be built on a commitment that both people understand and agree on.

Negative: But if people have different ideas, they might need to talk about it and find a middle ground.

Self-Reflection:

What do you want from commitment? How do you show that you are committed to someone?

Practical Guidance:

Explore what commitment means to both of you, including how you feel about each other, what goals you have in common, how loyal you are to each other, and what you do for each other. How does it show up in your daily lives, plans, or promises?

Talk about how your ideas about commitment are the same or different. How will you build commitment, show it, or talk about it in your relationship? What kinds of understanding, growth, or shared practices might be involved?

Think about what commitment means in your relationship as a whole. How will it change your relationship, happiness, or journey together? How will you honor, test, or grow your shared commitment?

Holistic Viewpoints:

The idea of commitment can be very personal and complex. It could include things like loyalty, honesty, communication, having the same goals, and for some, even making a sacrifice. For some, commitment means putting an emphasis on personal growth, independence within the relationship, or certain activities or rituals that both people do. Each person's idea of commitment is shaped by things like their culture, past relationships, personal experiences, and beliefs.

Not only do people have different "levels" of commitment, but they may also have very different ideas about what it means to be committed. Some might see it as a legal or religious obligation, while others might see it as a choice they make every day to put the relationship first. These differences don't always have to do with right and wrong, but they do show deeper values and ways of thinking.

This is why it's so important to approach this subject with an open mind and compassion. Conversations about commitment should go both ways, with both people talking about not only what commitment means but also why it means what it does. This makes the relationship stronger and makes sure that both people are on the same page, even if they have very different backgrounds.

For Long-term Relationships:

Commitment is not a fixed idea that stays the same from the first time two people get together. As a relationship grows and changes through different stages, like moving in together, getting married, having kids, changing jobs, or getting older, so does the way people understand and show their commitment. For instance, when a couple first starts dating, commitment might mean spending time together and getting to know each other.

In the future, it might be about helping each other with their careers or taking care of each other when they are sick.

At different points in a relationship, talking about what commitment means again makes sure that both partners continue to feel safe and valued. It's also a chance to notice and celebrate how both people and the relationship have grown.

Couples can make a stronger, more satisfying, and more real bond if they realize that commitment is complicated and can change over time. To do this, you need to talk to each other often, have empathy, and be willing to be open and honest about your changing feelings and needs.

In the end, the question of what commitment means comes down to what kind of relationship you want to build together, how you want to support each other, and how you'll handle the inevitable changes that life will bring. It's a key part of making a life together, and like everything else that's important, it needs time, attention, and care.

Expert Insight – Attachment Styles:

Secure Attachment Style: For people with this attachment style, commitment usually means a stable, reliable, and equal relationship where both people can depend on each other. Most of the time, people think of commitment as staying in a relationship even when there are problems, with the main goal being to work things out together.

Anxious Attachment Style: People with this style might think that being committed means being told over and over that they are loved and cared for. They might need to see signs of their partner's commitment over and over again before they feel safe in the relationship.

Avoidant Attachment Style: People with this style might think that commitment isn't as important as other things. They may like having their own space in a relationship and see commitment as a way to stay together without giving up their own freedom.

Disorganized Attachment Style: People with a disorganized attachment style can find it hard to understand commitment. They may want the security that comes with a commitment, but they may also be afraid of the openness it brings. Their ideas about commitment might change over time and seem to be at odds with each other.

Question #18:

What are your views on marriage?

Purpose:

To know how your partner feels about the idea of marriage. Do they want a Cinderella-style wedding, or are they more interested in a lifelong relationship without any paperwork?

Why It's Important:

Marriage views affect long-term relationship goals. Open dialogue helps align expectations.

Possible Answers:

- "I think getting married is a big step in life and a way to show commitment."

- "I do not think you need a legal contract to show that you love or care about someone."

Follow-up Questions:

- Do you want to get married in the future?

- How do you feel about non-traditional types of marriage or unions?

On a Lighter Note:

If they say, "Marriage is a workshop where one works and the other shops," then you might be dealing with a class clown, or they might need a crash course in equality and shared responsibilities!

Positive and Negative Aspects:

Positive: Getting on the same page about how important marriage is (or isn't) can help you and your partner stay on the same path.

Negative: But having different ideas could kill the deal.

Self-Reflection:

How do you feel about marriage? Is it an important part of a relationship, or do you see it differently?

Practical Guidance:

Talk about what marriage means to you both based on your cultural beliefs, personal values, or emotional significance. How does it match or differ from your own or your group's ideas about commitment, family, or partnerships?

Think about how you see, value, and approach marriage. How will you talk about, plan for, or work together on this part of your relationship? What kind of understanding, creativity, or shared journey might be involved?

Think about what marriage means for your relationship as a whole. How will it change your relationship, how you see yourselves together, or your long-term plans? How will you celebrate, test, or change your marriage?

Holistic Viewpoints:

Marriage is a topic about which people can have very different and deeply personal ideas. Some people think of marriage as a religious rite, while others might see it as a legal requirement or even an old-fashioned institution. These views are shaped in large part by cultural backgrounds, personal experiences, family traditions, and individual values.

When you and your partner talk about marriage, it's important to be aware of these differences. It's not enough to just agree or disagree; you also need to understand your partner's deeper values and beliefs. This understanding is based on empathy, an open mind, and listening with intent.

Ask your partner not only what they think about marriage, but why they think that way. Look into the experiences and values that led to these beliefs. This not only helps people understand each other better, but it can also reveal values and goals they share that might not be obvious at first.

For Long-term Relationships:

Not everyone has the same ideas about marriage. Those views might change as people grow and as their relationships change. Changes in how someone sees marriage could be caused by their life experiences, personal growth, and how their family is changing.

This is why it's important to have this conversation often, especially when big things happen in your life. It's not about persuading or bargaining. Instead, it's about always understanding where each person is in the relationship and what they want from it. It makes sure that both people stay on the same page and can handle changes together.

Keep in mind that a change in how you feel about marriage doesn't always mean there's something wrong with your relationship. It could just mean that the person has changed or learned more about what commitment means to them. Regular, understanding conversations can turn this potential source of conflict into a chance to connect and understand each other better.

Expert Insight:

Marriage is often seen as the highest level of commitment, especially in cultures that put a lot of emphasis on it. But researchers and relationship experts[1] often say that marriage isn't the only way to have a successful, long-term relationship.

---

1. https://www.thezoereport.com/wellness/long-term-relationship-with-no-marriage #:~:text=For%20some%20people%2C%20marriage%20isn,it%20%E2%80%94%20i f%20not%20more%20so.

The most important thing is that both people agree on what the relationship is and where it's going. Some couples might get married and take the same last name. For others, it could mean a committed partnership without a legal contract. Neither is better or worse in and of itself; what matters is that it reflects the values, goals, and desires of both partners.

At the end of the day, talking about marriage is really about what kind of life you want to make together. It takes empathy, honesty, openness, and a willingness to see and value your partner's unique point of view, just like any other meaningful conversation.

Question #19:

What do you think about staying together when things get hard? When, if ever, would you think about getting a divorce?

Purpose:

This question helps you figure out how strong and committed your partner is during hard times and what they think about ending a marriage. It is like asking, "Do you see your marriage as the Titanic or more like a Rubber Ducky in a storm?"

Why It's Important:

This can reveal a person's resilience in tough times and commitment to relationship maintenance.

Possible Answers:

- "Before thinking about divorce, I think it is best to work through problems and get help, like counseling."

- "I think divorce can be an option if there is a lot of bad behavior or problems that can not be solved."

Follow-up Questions:

- How would you handle things if our relationship got rough?

- How do you feel about marriage counseling or therapy?

On a Lighter Note:

If they say, "I'd only consider divorce if you stop laughing at my jokes," you might need to stock up on some laughing gas!

Positive and Negative Aspects:

Positive: It can be comforting to have a partner who is willing to work through problems with you.

Negative: But someone who sees divorce as an easy way out might not care as much about working things out.

Self-Reflection:

Think about your limits and what, if anything, would make you think about getting a divorce.

Practical Guidance:

Talk about how you think staying together through hard times shows your commitment, strength, or limits. What values, actions, or understandings help you both get through hard times?

Think about how you'd handle hard times or a possible divorce. How will you help, talk about, or deal with these things? What shared habits, therapy, or mutual respect might be involved?

Think about what resilience and time apart mean for your relationship as a whole. How will they affect your relationship, your growth together, or your long-term understanding? How will you work through, learn from, or grow from these things as a team?

Holistic Viewpoints:

Staying together during difficult times and considering divorce are deeply personal topics that may evoke strong emotions and convictions. People's beliefs on these matters are often rooted in their cultural background, religious faith, personal experiences, and the examples set by family and friends.

To engage in a meaningful conversation about these subjects with a partner, it's essential to approach the discussion with sensitivity, empathy, and care. Recognize that these are not simply abstract concepts but could relate to deeply held values and potentially painful experiences. It's not about reaching a definitive answer but understanding the complexities and nuances of each other's perspectives.

Rather than approaching this conversation as a debate or negotiation, try to explore it as a journey into understanding what commitment, resilience, and relationship success mean to both of you. By uncovering the underlying values and fears that shape your views, you may find new avenues for connection and empathy.

For Long-term Relationships:

As relationships progress and evolve, couples may face various challenges and hardships. It's natural and expected. But understanding how both partners view these challenges and what they see as grounds for staying together or considering divorce can be a vital part of building a resilient relationship.

This understanding isn't something that's established once and then forgotten. It may require ongoing conversation and reflection as life changes. What feels like an insurmountable obstacle early in a relationship might seem manageable later on, or vice versa.

What's crucial here is not to focus solely on the specifics of what might lead to divorce but to foster a shared understanding of what it means to face challenges together. Explore what support looks like, what trust means, and how you can communicate effectively even when things are hard.

By creating a shared narrative of resilience, growth, and partnership, couples can reinforce their connection and prepare to face whatever life throws their way. It's not about planning for failure but building the strength, understanding, and empathy that can make the relationship more robust.

Expert Insight – Attachment Styles:

Secure Attachment Style: People who are securely attached tend to have a positive view of relationships and think that people should stick together through hard times. After trying everything else to solve their problems, divorce is probably the last thing they will try.

Anxious Attachment Style: People with this style may not like the idea of a relationship ending and may hold on to it even when there are big problems. They might worry a lot about getting a divorce, and they might see every fight as a possible threat to their relationship.

Avoidant Attachment Style: People with this attachment style might think that hard times in a relationship are a sign that they should pull away or even end the relationship. They might not be as worried about getting a divorce because they like to be on their own and have their own space.

Disorganized Attachment Style: People with this style may have mixed feelings about staying together through hard times and thinking about getting a divorce. When things get hard, they may go back and forth between being afraid to end the relationship and wanting to get out of it.

Question #20:

What are your views on prenuptial agreements? Under what circumstances would you consider having one?

Purpose:

This question is a way to find out what your partner thinks about prenuptial agreements, which might not seem romantic but are important from a practical standpoint. It is not as romantic as proposing at sunset, but wouldn't it be even stranger to propose a prenup at sunset?

Why It's Important:

Discussing prenuptial agreements can provide insight into financial values and expectations for the relationship.

Possible Answers:

- "I think that prenuptial agreements are a good way to protect each person's assets."

- "I think that planning for a possible breakup can make a marriage more likely to fail."

Follow-up Questions:

- Would you consider getting a prenuptial agreement?

- What factors would influence your decision?

On a Lighter Note:

If they say, "I'd only sign a prenup if it stated that you'd never make me watch another romantic comedy," well, you might have to reevaluate your movie night choices!

Positive and Negative Aspects:

Positive: When a partner is willing to talk about prenuptial agreements, it shows that they are practical and responsible with money.

Negative: But if they think a prenup means they do not trust or care about each other, they might not be as practical or willing to talk about money.

Self-Reflection:

Think about how you feel about prenuptial agreements and when you might be interested in getting one.

Practical Guidance:

Talk about how you feel about prenuptial agreements, taking into account your financial security, your legal rights, or your own personal values. How do they match your shared beliefs, plans, or trust, or how do they differ?

Check out how you could approach or talk about a prenuptial agreement. How will you talk, make plans, or help each other through this? What might be involved in terms of understanding, empathy, or making decisions together?

Think about what a prenuptial agreement means for your relationship as a whole. How will it change your relationship, your trust in each other, or your long-term plans? How will you handle, respect, or fit this into the whole?

Holistic Viewpoints:

Prenuptial agreements are legal documents that say how the couple's assets will be split if they get divorced. People often look at them in different ways, depending on their own values, their culture, the law, or even their own feelings.

Some people may see a prenuptial agreement as a practical, smart step that takes into account the financial side of marriage. For others, it might seem like a lack of trust or a touchy subject that makes the relationship look bad.

When talking about this topic, it's important to remember that it's not just a legal or financial choice. It has a lot to do with what people believe, how much they trust each other, and what marriage means to them as a symbol. So, talking about prenuptial agreements should be done in an open, understanding, and non-judgmental way.

Understanding where your partner is coming from, why they have the views they do, and what fears or hopes they have about a prenuptial agreement can help you have a more nuanced conversation that respects both partners' feelings.

For Long-term Relationships:

Relationships that last for a long time can make things even more complicated. As a couple gets to know each other better and their finances change, their views on prenuptial agreements may also change. Prenuptial agreements can be replaced or added to by cohabitation agreements or postnuptial agreements for people who don't plan to get married or who are already married.

By talking about and reviewing these agreements often, you can make sure they are still useful and fair. Less attention should be paid to the details of the legal agreement and more to the underlying principles that guide how you handle money, assets, and responsibilities in the relationship.

Having these talks can also be a way to talk about bigger issues in the relationship, like money, trust, and working together. Instead of being a one-time decision, it can be part of an ongoing conversation that strengthens the emotional and financial bond between partners.

Expert Insight:

Legal experts often talk about the practical benefits of prenuptial agreements, especially for people who have significant assets or children from previous relationships. But they also warn that these agreements should be thought about and made with care and fairness to keep people from getting hurt or stressed out more than they need to.

A well-written prenuptial agreement can make things clear and help avoid disagreements in the future. But this must be weighed against the possible emotional effects and the need to make sure that the agreement reflects the shared values and goals of the relationship.

If you decide to go this route, it might be smart to hire a lawyer who knows the law and can give you advice based on your situation.

Question #21:

How do you feel about renewing our wedding vows?

Purpose:

With this question, you can find out what your partner thinks about the idea of renewing your wedding vows. It is a great way to find out if they want to relive the magic of your wedding day or if they think it is like rewatching a movie they have already seen, albeit one with a great ending.

Why It's Important:

This question can reveal a person's views on relationship milestones and romantic gestures.

Possible Answers:

- "I love the idea of reminding ourselves of the promise we made."

- "I do not think it is necessary; once it is done, it should be done for good."

Follow-up Questions:

- Under what circumstances would you consider renewing our vows?

- Do you think it's important to do it in a special location, or is the act itself enough?

On a Lighter Note:

Imagine them saying, "I'd renew our vows, but only if we can do it at the end of a Star Trek convention!" Beam me up, Scotty!

Positive and Negative Aspects:

Positive: If your partner is open to the idea of renewing vows, they might be the type who likes romantic gestures and the symbolic confirmation of commitment.

Negative: On the other hand, if they do not want it, they might be more practical and think that the original vows are enough and will last.

Self-Reflection:

Think about how you feel about renewing your vows. Are you interested in the idea? If so, under what conditions would you do it?

Practical Guidance:

Talk about what renewing your wedding vows means to you both in terms of your romantic feelings, shared milestones, or personal beliefs. How does it fit with or enhance your emotional connection, shared memories, or relationship growth?

Explore how you see, value, or approach renewing vows. How will you plan, celebrate, or share this part of your relationship? What kind of creativity, joy, or shared expression might be involved?

Think about the bigger meaning of renewing your vows in your relationship. How will it make your connection, shared journey, or long-term fulfillment better? How will you embrace, honor, or change this aspect together?

Holistic Viewpoints:

The idea of renewing wedding vows can have a lot of emotional and symbolic weight. Some people might think it's a beautiful way to show their love and commitment, while others might think it's unnecessary or even uncomfortable.

It is important to understand and respect these different points of view. Some people might think that renewing vows is romantic and has a lot of meaning. They might see it as a chance to show their love and commitment in public.

Others might think that their original vows are sacred and will never change and that renewing them would make them less important. They might prefer to show their continued commitment in private or through other actions and gestures that mean a lot.

The point is that there is no one right or wrong way to renew your wedding vows. It's about understanding what it means to both partners and finding a way to honor those feelings, whether through a formal ceremony or other ways of showing commitment.

For Long-term Relationships:

In long-term relationships, the idea of renewing vows or reaffirming commitment might come up after reaching certain milestones, getting through hard times, or just as a spontaneous way to show how much love has grown over time.

This doesn't have to be a formal ceremony where you say your vows again. Some couples might want a quiet, private reaffirmation, a special trip together, or a unique gift that represents their relationship.

The key is to talk about what commitment and affirmation mean in the relationship on a regular basis and make sure that both partners are happy with the method chosen. It's not a one-time decision, but rather an ongoing conversation that shows how long-term relationships change over time.

Expert Insight:

Relationship experts often promote vow renewals as a positive practice[2]. They can provide a couple with an opportunity to reflect on their journey, celebrate their growth, and look forward to their future together. Such a ceremony can also act as a healing or strengthening moment, especially if the relationship has faced significant challenges.

---

2. Braithwaite, D. O. (2003). Renewal of wedding vows. In J. J. Ponzetti (Ed.), The international encyclopedia of marriage and the family relationships (2nd. ed.).

However, it's important to note that a vow renewal should be a mutual decision and something that aligns with both partners' feelings and beliefs. The ceremony or act itself is less important than the shared understanding and intention behind it.

Experts also emphasize that renewing vows is not a fix for underlying relationship problems. It can be a symbol of love and commitment but should not replace ongoing communication, mutual respect, and the daily efforts that make a relationship thrive.

Question #22:

How have past relationships shaped your views on love and commitment?

Purpose:

To know how your partner's past relationships have changed the way they think about love, commitment, and relationships in general.

Why it's Important:

Relationships from the past have a similar effect on us. They can affect how we start new relationships, handle disagreements, and show love and commitment.

Possible Answers:

- "My past relationships taught me the importance of open communication, trust, and patience in maintaining love and commitment."

- "I've learned that love requires effort and mutual respect to foster commitment."

Follow-Up Questions:

- What did you learn about what works and what doesn't in a relationship?

- How do these experiences influence your approach to our relationship?

On a Lighter Note:

"So, has your ex set the bar so low that I've already surpassed it?"

Positive and Negative Aspects:

Positive: This conversation gives both sides a chance to learn from each other's experiences and use what they have learned to build a stronger relationship.

Negative: Thinking about old relationships could bring up painful memories or feelings that have not been dealt with.

Self-Reflection:

Think about your past relationships. How did they change the way you think about love and commitment?

Practical Guidance:

Talk about how the relationships you've had in the past have shaped, changed, or reinforced your ideas about love and commitment. Focus on understanding, empathy, self-awareness, or resilience as you look at the values, lessons, insights, or growth that these experiences have given you.

Explore how you and your partner will incorporate, honor, or learn from these experiences in your relationship, which will help you both understand each other better, connect, trust each other more, or grow.

Exercise: Have a conversation in which you share the most important lessons you've learned from past relationships and how they've changed the way you think about love and commitment now.

Holistic Viewpoints:

Understanding a partner's past requires a careful and thoughtful look at many things, such as their culture, socioeconomic background, health history, family dynamics, and even past traumas. These parts of a person's life may affect what they believe, what they value, how they act, and how they feel. When talking about these topics, you need to be careful, have empathy, and be aware that the information might be sensitive.

Communication that is respectful and kind creates a safe space where partners feel comfortable talking about their pasts.

For Long-term Relationships:

People who have been together for a long time often know a lot about each other's pasts. But some areas may not be explored or shared because they were missed or because they were kept secret on purpose. By constantly working to create a trusting and nonjudgmental space, partners can feel safe talking about more personal or hard parts of their pasts. This kind of sharing can deepen emotional closeness and make connections stronger.

Expert Insight – Attachment Styles:

Studies, like the one done by Alea and Vick[3], show that knowing and understanding your partner's past experiences can make your relationship happier and more stable. It helps people feel more empathy, compassion, and connection. But it's important to know how the different types of attachment can affect this process:

Secure Attachment Style: People with this attachment style are usually open and don't mind talking about their past, which makes it easier to understand each other.

Anxious Attachment Style: People with this style may feel a strong need to talk about their past, but they may also be afraid of being rejected or judged. They may need extra reassurance and understanding.

Avoidant Attachment Style: People with this style may not want to talk about their past because they value independence and privacy. Trust and gradual sharing can grow with patience and gentle encouragement.

Disorganized Attachment Style: This style of attachment could lead to inconsistent or confusing ways of talking about personal history, which could be a sign of fears or

---

3. Alea, N., & Vick, S. C. (2010). The first sight of love: Relationship-defining memories and marital satisfaction across adulthood

trauma that hasn't been dealt with. To deal with this complicated situation, you may need sensitivity and/or help from a professional.

Question #23:

What are your thoughts on divorce? How do you view it as an option in a marriage?

Purpose:

The goal is to find out what your partner thinks, feels, and thinks about divorce. Is it the very last option? An acceptable choice in some situations? Or is it something else?

Why it's important:

Talking about how you feel about divorce helps you understand each other's expectations and limits in the marriage. It can also show what values, beliefs, and experiences lie behind these points of view.

Possible Answers:

- "Divorce is something I hope to never have to think about, but I know there are times when it might be the best choice."

- "I think divorce is a very serious and permanent choice that should only be made when all other options have been tried and failed."

Follow-up Questions:

- What do you think about counseling or mediation for couples?

- What do you think would be a reason for us to end our marriage?

- What can we do to keep from getting to the point where we might think about getting a divorce?

On a Lighter Note:

If they say, "Divorce is never an option, but I'll fight you for the remote control," it's a funny way to lighten up a serious subject.

Positive and Negative Aspects:

Positive: Talking about divorce in an open and honest way can make the relationship stronger by making sure expectations are clear and fostering understanding.

Negative: Differences of opinion may go back a long way and be hard to solve.

Self-Reflection:

How do you feel about divorce on a personal level? Have past events or cultural beliefs changed the way you look at things? What are the things you can't live without in a relationship that might make you think about getting a divorce?

Practical Guidance:

It's a good idea to talk about how you feel about divorce before you get married or early in your relationship. During this talk, you might talk about specific situations, like cheating or not being responsible with money, and how you and your partner would handle them.

Be honest and open with each other, and approach the conversation with empathy and respect, keeping in mind that these are deeply personal and possibly sensitive topics.

Holistic Viewpoints:

People's ideas about divorce are often complicated and shaped by things like culture, religion, personal experiences, and family history. They can show deeper values like commitment, personal growth, integrity, and the ability to bounce back from hard times.

It's important to approach the topic with understanding and an open mind, knowing that people's ideas about divorce can be very different and personal. The goal shouldn't be to convince or judge, but to understand each other's point of view.

For Long-Term Relationships:

Talking early on about how each person feels about divorce can set the stage for open communication and problem-solving in the future. Regular check-ins and honest conversations can help a couple work through problems before they get so bad that they might think about getting a divorce.

Expert Insight – Attachment Styles:

Secure Attachment Style: Sees divorce as a last resort, values stability, and partnership, and is willing to work through problems together.

Anxious Attachment Style: May worry about being left alone or rejected, which can make them feel very strongly about divorce.

Avoidant Attachment Style: If you have an avoidant attachment style, you might think that divorce is the only way to keep your personal freedom or control.

Disorganized Attachment Style: They may have mixed feelings about divorce because their relationship with commitment and attachment is complicated.

Overall, talking about divorce isn't about making plans for failure; it's about learning what each other values and expects. As long as the conversation is handled with care, empathy, and an open mind, it can be a way to get closer and build trust.

Question #24:

Have you experienced divorce within your family or close circle? How has that influenced your perspective?

Purpose:

The goal is to talk about any divorces in your family or close circle of friends and find out how those divorces have changed your partner's view of divorce.

Why it's important:

A person's own divorce can have a big effect on how they think about marriage, commitment, and the possibility of divorce. This question gives you the chance to learn more about your partner's thoughts and feelings about those experiences.

Possible Answers:

- "When I was young, my parents did get a divorce. It was a hard time. It has made me want to work through problems in a relationship even more."

- "No, my family hasn't gone through a divorce, but a close friend has, and it taught me how important it is to talk to people."

Follow-up Questions:

- How did the divorce change the way you talk to your family or friends?

- What did you learn from seeing someone get divorced?

- How can we use what we've learned to make our relationship better?

On a Lighter Note:

If they say, "No divorces, but lots of fights over who gets the last piece of cake!" it adds a bit of humor to a serious conversation.

Positive and Negative Aspects:

Positive: Understanding how your partner's past divorce experiences have changed how they see things can deepen empathy and connection.

Negative: This talk might bring up painful memories or strong feelings.

Self-reflection:

Have you or someone close to you been through a divorce? How has that changed how you feel about marriage and divorce? What can you learn from those things that will help you and your partner get closer?

Practical Guidance:

Be ready for emotional reactions and be aware of how your partner feels. Don't judge or offer solutions; instead, offer support and understanding.

Use this conversation to talk about the values and commitments you both share and to find ways to take care of and protect your relationship.

Holistic Viewpoints:

Divorce in a family or close group of friends can change the way people think about relationships, commitment, trust, and being strong. These influences can be very different. For example, they might emphasize how important loyalty and persistence are or how important personal growth and independence are.

To understand these influences, you need to have compassion and talk about them openly, while keeping in mind that they are often very personal and tied to a lot of different feelings and memories.

For long-term relationships:

Talking about your partner's past divorces, even if it hurts, can help you understand their values, fears, and expectations. Regularly talking about these things can make your relationship stronger and help you deal with any problems that might come up.

Expert Insight – Attachment Styles:

Secure Attachment Style: Likely to approach the subject with empathy and logic, seeing it as a chance to learn and grow.

Anxious Attachment Style: They may feel threatened or upset, and they need to be reassured and understood.

Avoidant Attachment Style: The person might brush off the subject or try to avoid it, so they need patience and gentle probing.

Disorganized Attachment Style: Could have conflicting feelings that need to be navigated carefully and helped with.

Talking about one's own divorce can be powerful and enlightening, but it can also be very emotional. Approaching the topic with sensitivity, empathy, and a real desire to understand can lead to a deeper connection and more trust.

Question #25:

How do you envision handling financial matters and responsibilities in case of separation or divorce?

Purpose:

The goal is to find out what your partner thinks and expects about how to handle money and responsibilities in case you break up or divorce.

Why it's Important:

Even though it's a sensitive and maybe even uncomfortable subject, talking about financial responsibilities in case of a breakup or divorce lets both partners be on the same page and plan for any unexpected events that might happen. It also builds trust and openness by showing that you can talk openly about hard things.

Possible Answers:

- "I think assets should be divided fairly based on what we've contributed and what's legal."

- "I would hope that we could work it out in a way that respects each other's needs and keeps the peace."

Follow-up Questions:

- What do you think about prenuptial agreements?

- What do you think is a fair way to split up a marriage?

- What values or rules guide the way you think about this?

On a Lighter Note:

If they say, "Let's make a deal: whoever leaves pays the bills!" it might be a way to add humor to a serious conversation, but it's worth looking into more.

Positive and Negative Aspects:

Positive: Talking about this openly can make people less worried about the unknown and build trust.

Negative: It can be hard and awkward to talk about, and it might bring up fears or worries.

Self-Reflection:

What do you think about how to handle money in the event of a breakup or divorce? How do your ideas match or clash with those of your partner?

Practical Guidance:

Approach the conversation with sensitivity and respect, keeping in mind that it may bring up discomfort or strong emotions.

Make it clear that this is just a made-up scenario and that the goal is to get to know each other better, not to look into the future or predict what will happen.

Holistic Viewpoints:

This conversation is about more than just money. It is also about deeper values like fairness, responsibility, trust, and commitment. It's about knowing how each other thinks and how each of you would handle a hard or painful situation.

For Long-Term Relationships:

As a relationship develops, financial situations may change. Talking about this topic regularly can make sure that everyone is still on the same page and understands what's going on.

Consider getting professional help, like legal or financial counseling, so you can talk about your options and their effects in a safe place.

Expert Insight – Attachment Styles:

Secure Attachment Style: Likely to approach this subject calmly, thinking of it as part of responsible planning.

Anxious Attachment Style: May feel insecure or threatened by the topic and needs reassurance of commitment.

Avoidant Attachment Style: The person might find the subject uncomfortable or unimportant, and they might need a gentle push to get involved.

Disorganized Attachment Style: Could act in ways you couldn't predict, so you had to be careful.

In case of separation or divorce, it can be hard to talk about money because it can touch on deeply held beliefs and feelings. It's best to talk about it carefully, with an open mind, and with the goal of understanding and respecting each other's points of view. It's not about predicting something bad will happen, but about preparing in a responsible and open way.

CHAPTER FIVE

CHILDREN

NAVIGATING THE JOYS AND CHALLENGES OF PARENTHOOD

Question #26:

How many children do you want, if any?

Purpose:

This question is about one of the most important things for a couple to talk about: whether or not to have kids and, if so, how many. It is a key part of understanding how you see the future together.

Why It's Important:

Discussions on family planning are vital to align expectations and plans for the future.

Possible Answers:

- "I want kids for sure, preferably two or three."

- "I am open to having kids, but I do not have to."

- "I would rather not have kids."

Follow-up Questions:

- What makes you think that way about having kids?

- How do you see our lives going if you get the number of kids you want?

- What do you think about adopting or fostering a child if we cannot have our own?

On a Lighter Note:

If they want a big family, get ready to step on Legos and live in a living room that is always a mess. But hey, at least you'll have an in-built team for all board games!

Positive and Negative Aspects:

Positive: If you both want the same number of kids, it can make your relationship stronger and help you plan for the future.

Negative: On the other hand, if there is a mismatch in this area, it could lead to major disagreements and require a lot of compromising.

Self-Reflection:

Think about what you want and what worries you have about having kids. Is there room for compromise, and what will not you give up on?

Practical Guidance:

Start by having an honest conversation about whether or not you both want kids. If both partners agree that they want children, talk about what that means for each of you. Explore the reasons behind the number of children you want and what that might mean for your lifestyle, finances, and values.

Keep in mind that your personal, health, or financial situation could affect this decision in the future. Flexibility can be very important here, so talk about things that could happen that might make you have to change your plans, like problems with fertility or a change in career or location.

You could also talk about the timing. When do you plan on starting a family? How might this fit with other life goals or career plans? Are there any big goals or achievements you both want to reach before having kids?

If one partner wants kids and the other doesn't, or if there's a big difference in the number of kids each wants, it might be helpful to talk about this with the help of a relationship counselor. This is a very personal and sometimes emotionally charged topic. Getting help from a professional can help you have these conversations with care and understanding.

In future talks, you might also talk about the children's education, parenting styles, dividing up responsibilities, and help from extended family.

Holistic Viewpoints:

Not all couples can or choose to have biological children. Options like adoption, fostering, or not having children are equally valid choices for family life.

For Long-term Relationships:

This conversation is often very important in long-term relationships and may need to be had more than once as things change. Fertility, health, financial stability, career goals, and other things in your life can change or change how you feel about planning a family. By talking about these things all the time, both partners can make sure they are on the same page and working toward the same goals.

Question #27:

What parenting style do you believe in?

Purpose:

This question lets you know what your partner thinks about how to raise children. It will help you figure out how they might handle discipline, responsibility, and taking care of children if you decide to have kids together.

Why It's Important:

Knowing your partner's parenting beliefs can help avoid conflicts and ensure you're on the same page when it comes to raising children.

Possible Answers:

- "I believe in the authoritative style, in which I keep rules and freedom in balance."

- "I am more of a free-spirited person. I think kids learn best when there are not too many distractions."

- "I think rules and structure are important in an authoritarian style."

Follow-up Questions:

- Can you give some examples of how you would deal with different parenting situations?

- How did you grow up, and how did that shape your ideas about how to raise children?

- What part do you see yourself playing in our child's education and activities outside of school?

On a Lighter Note:

If they tend toward the authoritarian style, get ready to run a boot camp at home with a perfectly organized toy rack. But don't worry, you'll always know where to find that missing puzzle piece.

Positive and Negative Aspects:

Positive: Matching parenting styles can make it easier to raise children in a way that is consistent, which can reduce conflict and confusion.

Negative: Discrepancies, on the other hand, may require negotiation and compromise.

Self-Reflection:

What is your preferred parenting style? Can you match your parenting styles so that your kids grow up in a consistent, safe place?

Practical Guidance:

Start this conversation by talking about how you were raised by your parents. Then discuss what you each think makes a family environment that is healthy and helpful. You could think about what you've seen with other children in your family or community while growing up. What did you like and what did you not like about those things? What would you want to do again or stay away from?

Talk about things like discipline, education, setting limits, and nurturing to learn more about your partner's parenting beliefs and values. Remember that it's not enough to agree or disagree; it's also important to understand the ideas and feelings that lead to these opinions.

Remember that parenting is not static; it changes as children grow and as parents learn and adapt. Be willing to change your ideas about parenting as you gain more experience or face new challenges. Stress how important it is for parents to talk to each other often and help each other make decisions.

Know that there may be disagreements, and that's okay. Instead of trying to change each other's minds, try to understand each other's points of view. If you and your partner have very different ideas about how to raise children, you might want to get professional advice or read books about parenting to learn about different approaches. Participating in parenting classes or workshops is another positive and proactive way to get your parenting style on track.

Think about how your parenting style might fit in with your larger life goals, your career, your relationships with extended family, and the way you like to live. All of these things are connected and can change how you and your partner parent.

Lastly, don't forget that you are all on the same team. Parenting is a job that both parents have to do, and a united front is often better. Keep the lines of communication open, talk about how you feel and what worries you, and be willing to change and grow together.

Examples of Parenting Styles:

- **Authoritative**: This style is characterized by a high level of responsiveness and high expectations. Parents who are authoritative have clear rules, but they also let their kids do some things on their own, talk to them openly, and are caring and warm.

- **Authoritarian**: This style makes a lot of demands but doesn't listen much. When parents are too strict, they expect their children to do what they say without asking why. They are less willing to negotiate, and rules are more important to them than being friendly or talking to people.

- **Permissive**: This style is characterized by high responsiveness and low demands. Most permissive parents are kind and generous, but they don't give their kids many rules or expectations. They try to avoid fights and give their kids a lot of freedom most of the time.

- **Uninvolved**: This style doesn't expect much and doesn't get much in return. Parents who aren't involved may be neglectful because they don't ask much of their kids, talk to them much, or care for them.

Question #28:

How will we handle decisions about our children's education?

Purpose:

The goal here is to find out what your partner thinks about education and what he or she wants for your future kids. You should also think about how decisions might be made in this important area of your kids' lives.

Why It's Important:

Decisions about children's education can impact their future and require joint planning and agreement.

Possible Answers:

- "I think a balanced approach is best. We should talk and make decisions together."

- "I think we should take turns leading, depending on who knows more about that subject."

Follow-up Questions:

- What role do you think parents should play in a child's education?

- What do you think about public vs. private schools?

On a Lighter Note:

"Well, if Hogwarts sends an acceptance letter, we're definitely saying yes!"

Positive and Negative Aspects:

Positive: A partner who wants to work together on decisions about education shows that they want a balanced partnership.

Negative: On the other hand, if they insist on making all the decisions themselves, it could show that they like to be in charge.

Self-Reflection:

Think about how you want to learn and what you value. How open are you to talking about these things and making deals?

Practical Guidance:

Making decisions about your child's education can be a difficult and important part of being a parent. It shows how you and your child share values, goals, and responsibilities.

Talk about your beliefs, values, and priorities when it comes to your children's education. Think about things like school choices, your educational philosophy, extracurricular activities, and long-term goals. Know how your shared or different beliefs, cultural backgrounds, or personal experiences might affect these decisions.

Focus on communication, shared decision-making, research, or family involvement as you think about how you will make and negotiate decisions about your children's education. How will you deal with different points of view, the needs of your family, or money issues? What kind of planning, working together, or feeling for each other might be involved?

Holistic Viewpoints:

Education for children is not a one-size-fits-all situation. Even though traditional schooling is common, it may not be right for every child. Being open to different ways of teaching, like homeschooling, Montessori, or Waldorf, as a parent can help you find a better way to meet your child's needs.

Understanding Your Child's Needs: Every child is different, and so may have different educational needs. It might be helpful to talk to teachers or educational psychologists to find out what kind of learning environment would be best for your child.

Exploring Options: Whether it's specialized schools, online learning, or homeschooling, looking into other options for your child's education could help him or her grow in a better way. Parents can learn a lot from doing research, visiting schools, and talking to other parents who have made similar choices.

Aligning Values and Goals: Education isn't just about learning facts; it's also about teaching values, social skills, and life philosophies. Finding a way to learn that fits with the core beliefs of your family can make for a more peaceful upbringing.

For Long-term Relationships:

If you've been with the same person for a while and already have kids, the way you make decisions about their education may change over time.

Reviewing Previous Decisions: As children grow, their needs and interests change, as well as the family's situation. Reviewing your educational choices on a regular basis will help you keep up with how things are changing.

Communication Between Partners: Making decisions about education doesn't happen just once. It takes ongoing communication between partners to make sure that decisions are still in the best interests of the child and family.

Including Children in Decisions: Depending on how old and mature the children are, including them in talks about their education can give them more power and help them feel more responsible.

Question #29:

How do you plan to discipline our children?

Purpose:

This question helps you find out what your partner thinks about how to discipline children and how they do it.

Why it's Important:

Keeping rules the same is the key to giving kids a stable, safe place to live. It is important to agree on how to discipline the child to avoid fights and make sure the child is healthy.

Possible Answers:

- "I believe in constructive discipline where we guide and teach rather than punish."

- "Setting clear expectations and consequences, and being consistent, is my approach to discipline."

On a Lighter Note:

"Remember, kids are like pancakes. We're bound to mess up the first one...I'm kidding! Or am I?"

Follow-Up Questions:

- What principles or values will guide your approach to discipline?

- How would you handle disagreements about discipline between us?

Positive and Negative Aspects:

Positive: You learn more about how your partner raises their kids and can talk with them about what works best for your family.

Negative: Different ideas about how to raise children can lead to conflict. It might take some time and honest talk to find a place where everyone can agree.

Self-Reflection:

Reflect on your own views of child discipline. Do you like time-outs, taking away privileges, logical consequences, or something else?

Practical Guidance:

Talk about your ideas, strategies, or values about how to discipline kids, with a focus on consistency, respect, setting limits, empathy, or working together. Find out how these ideas match or don't match those of your partner.

Find out how you and your partner will get along, work together, or help each other when it comes to disciplining children, building shared understanding, consistency, trust, or working together.

Exercise: Think about making a shared "discipline philosophy" that outlines the ways, values, and expectations that everyone agrees on.

Holistic Viewpoints:

When talking about child discipline, it's important to remember that people's views are shaped by their own cultures and experiences:

Different cultures may have different ways of raising children and ways to discipline them. Understanding these things can help people treat each other with respect.

Personal experiences, both good and bad, with discipline, can have a big effect on how parents think about it now. Open conversation can help bring these different experiences together into a single plan.

Every child is different, and their needs and responses to discipline can be different, too. A flexible approach that takes each child's personality and level of development into account can be helpful.

For Long-term Relationships:

In long-term relationships, especially those with children, it's important to talk about discipline all the time:

Consistency: Both parents should try to be consistent in how they discipline their kids, because sending them mixed messages can be confusing for them.

Evaluating How Well It Works: Check in on how well the chosen strategies are working every so often and make changes as needed.

Changes in life, like a new sibling, a new school, or other things, may mean that the way you discipline your child needs to change.

Expert Insight:

Expert opinions and research point to some core ideas[1] :

Positive Discipline: Rather than punishing, strategies that focus on teaching and guiding are often more effective in the long run.

Balance with warmth: Love, warmth, and understanding should go along with discipline for a good relationship between a parent and child.

Long-Term Effects: It is important to think about how different ways of disciplining a child might affect his or her future behavior, academic performance, and mental health.

---

1. https://www.health.harvard.edu/blog/the-better-way-to-discipline-children-2019 010115578

CHAPTER SIX

FAMILY

THE TIES THAT BIND - INTEGRATING FAMILY DYNAMICS

Question #30:

How important is it for you to maintain a close relationship with your family?

Purpose:

This question lets you know what your partner thinks about family and relationships. It is important to understand these values because they can affect many parts of your shared life, like how much time you spend with your family, how you spend your holidays, and even how you raise your children.

Why It's Important:

This provides insight into a person's family dynamics and values and can impact family interactions and time spent with family.

Possible Answers:

- "My family is important to me, and I like to keep in touch with them."

- "I maintain a healthy relationship with them, but I also value my independence."

- "I'm not very close with my family for personal reasons."

Follow-up Questions:

- How often do you like to visit your family?

- What is your overall relationship with family members?

- How might your family ties affect our relationship?

On a Lighter Note:

If your partner's family lives in a remote corner of Alaska, you might want to invest in a good winter jacket and bear-repellant. On the bright side, you will have a great reason not to go to those awkward holiday parties!

Positive and Negative Aspects:

Positive: Strong family ties can lead to a strong support system, which is a good thing.

Negative: On the other hand, too much family involvement can sometimes get in the way of a couple's independence.

Self-Reflection:

Consider your own family relationships as well as your level of comfort with your partner's family dynamics. Do you need to talk about any potential conflicts or synergies?

Practical Guidance:

First, it's important for each partner to talk about what "close" means to them. For some, this could mean daily phone calls or frequent visits, while for others, it could mean less frequent contact. Explore how you feel and what you want from your family, and be aware that you and your partner may have different ideas.

Talk about how your family worked in the past and how it works now to set the scene. Sharing stories about your childhood and how you get along with your family members now can help you figure out what you want and what you need.

Find out if there are any limits or worries that could come up with family involvement. This could mean talking about holidays, family traditions, or how much family members have an effect on personal choices. By being clear about what you want and what you won't do, you can avoid misunderstandings in the future.

Know that these feelings and needs may change over time, especially when big things happen in your life, like getting married, having kids, or going through a family crisis. Keep talking to each other so you can adjust to these changes and help each other's relationships with family members change.

If there are big disagreements or worries about family relationships, you might want to get help from a professional, such as through couples therapy. A neutral third party can help family members talk to each other in a healthy way and give them tools to deal with their complicated relationships.

Holistic Viewpoints:

Different cultures, personalities, and life experiences give different weight and importance to family relationships. Some people may see family ties as an important part of who they are and how they feel, while others may have more complicated or distant family relationships because of things like personal values, the way their family works, or bad experiences in the past. To understand a partner's family ties, you need to have empathy and be willing to look beyond the obvious.

Expert Insight:

Experts on relationships often talk about how a person's family relationships affect their overall happiness and, by extension, their romantic relationships. The way a person interacts with his or her family may show broader patterns of attachment, communication, and dealing with conflicts. When you talk openly about family ties, you can find out what values you share or where you might have problems. Therapy or counseling can also help if different ideas about family are making the relationship difficult.

Question #31:

Would you be okay if I have a very close relationship with my family?

Purpose:

This question is meant to find out how your partner feels about your close family ties. Knowing how they feel about it will help you avoid misunderstandings or fights in the future.

Why It's Important: This indicates their comfort level with your close family bonds and their adaptability to your family dynamics.

Possible Answers:

- "Yes, I like and respect family ties that are strong."

- "That depends on how it affects our relationship and how much time we have for ourselves."

- "I might have a hard time with it if it seems like they are getting in the way of our lives."

Follow-up Questions:

- Have you ever dated someone who was very close to their family? How did it affect you?

- What limits do you think should be put on how family members can help?

- Can we talk about how much time we spend with my family and find a middle ground?

On a Lighter Note:

"If you're concerned about me being too close with my family, don't worry – we mostly bond over game nights. But be warned, if you join us, you might just leave with an unexpected talent for Pictionary. And before you know it, you'll be the one everyone wants on their team for Charades!"

Positive and Negative Aspects:

Positive: One good thing is that they might respect the strong family values you have.

Negative: But they might also feel overwhelmed if it seems like your family is always around.

Self-Reflection:

Think about how your family works and how it has affected your past relationships. How can you balance the needs of your relationship with those of your close family?

Practical Guidance:

Start by telling them what it means to you to have a "close relationship" with your family. Are phone calls every day the norm? Do you plan on spending the holidays with each other? The better your partner can know what to expect from this close relationship, the more details you can give about it.

It could be helpful to think about how this relationship might affect your partner as well. Is there room for change if it goes against family traditions or their own needs? Understanding each other's comfort levels can help you find a balance between your family ties and your relationship.

Talk about things that could go wrong, like when family time and couple time clash. By talking about these possibilities up front, you can make plans for how to handle them if they happen.

It's also important to remember that both feelings and situations can change. Depending on how the relationship with the family changes, what seems okay now might not seem so good in the future. Keep the lines of communication open and check in often to make sure everyone's needs and feelings are still being taken into account.

For Long-term Relationships:

In long-term relationships, how you feel about being close to your family can affect how you spend the holidays, how much your family is involved in your life, and even the decisions you make every day. It's important to talk about and agree on how family relationships will fit into your life as a couple while respecting each other's limits and choices.

Expert Insight:

Relationship experts often talk about how important it is for family relationships to be honest and talk to each other. A close relationship between a partner and their family may bring joy and support, but it could also cause problems or make the other partner feel left out. Talking about expectations, limits, and the role of family in your relationship can help you both understand each other better and stop fights in the future.

Counselors also say that how a partner reacts to your relationship with your family can tell you about their own values, insecurities, and expectations. If you have a lot of worries, it might help to talk to a professional about how to handle these potentially sensitive issues.

Understanding and respecting each other's families and how they fit into your relationship can help make your relationship stronger and more balanced. Both partners' feelings and needs need to be taken into account and talked about in a way that makes the relationship stronger.

Question #32:

Are there any family traditions you want to continue?

Purpose:

This question is meant to help you find out what family traditions your partner loves and wants to keep going.

Why it's Important:

Each family has its own traditions, and those traditions are a big part of who we are as people. They show a person's background and who they are. By learning about them, you can find out more about your partner's past and what they value.

Possible Answers:

- "Yes, my family has a tradition of gathering for a big meal every Sunday, and I'd love to continue that."

- "Not particularly, but I'm open to creating new traditions together."

Follow-Up Questions:

- Can you tell me more about these traditions and why they're important to you?

- How would you feel about integrating our families' traditions?

On a Lighter Note:

"Okay, so you're telling me that your family dresses up as gnomes every midsummer night and dances around the backyard bonfire? That's...uhh...interesting!"

Positive and Negative Aspects:

Positive: Finding out that you and your partner share traditions or are interested in each other's customs can make your relationship even stronger.

Negative: If some of your partner's family traditions are strange or make you feel uncomfortable, you may need to talk to them and find a middle ground.

Self-Reflection:

Think about which of your family's traditions you really want to keep going and why. Are there any that you would rather not do?

Practical Guidance:

Talk about how family traditions have affected you, what you need, what you value, or how you feel. Focusing on heritage, connection, meaning, or authenticity can help you figure out what drives, shapes, or tests your connection to family traditions.

Think about how you will deal with, honor, or include family traditions in your relationship. Think about ways to create an atmosphere that fits with your heritage, values, connections, or identities as it relates to family traditions.

Exercise: Write down important family traditions from both sides and look for ways to honor, combine, or make new traditions that show how your shared values and connections fit together.

Holistic Viewpoints:

People often have a special place in their hearts for family traditions because they remind them of shared experiences, values, and history. But it's fine and normal if someone doesn't have any family traditions or would rather make their own. People's feelings about family traditions can be very different, depending on things like their cultural background, personal beliefs, the way their family works, or their own life experiences. Some people love and want to pass down their family traditions, while others may choose to break away from certain traditions or make new ones that fit with their life and values now.

For Long-term Relationships:

When people have been together for a long time, they talk about family traditions in a more nuanced way. Partners may come from different places and have different traditions, or they may come from the same place and have the same ones. When deciding what to keep, what to mix, and what to start from scratch, it's important to talk and negotiate. Respect for each other's history and a willingness to find a way forward together are very important. This can be a rewarding trip that brings people closer together and helps them feel like they belong to the same group. It also means noticing and respecting how these traditions make you feel, whether they bring you joy, comfort, or maybe even pain.

Expert Insight:

Research shows that family rituals and traditions are important for people's mental health. The same study by Fiese et al.[1] in the Journal of Family Psychology shows that these kinds of activities can help keep families together and help children feel emotionally healthy. These rituals give people a sense of continuity, stability, and belonging. They also connect people from different generations. They can be very important in shaping a family's identity and values, and they provide a structure that makes it easier for family members to feel close to each other.

---

1. Fiese, B. H., Tomcho, T. J., Douglas, M., Josephs, K., Poltrock, S., & Baker, T. (2002). A review of 50 years of research on naturally occurring family routines and rituals: Cause for celebration? Journal of Family Psychology, 16(4), 381–390.

Question #33:

What kind of relationship do you want with your in-laws?

Purpose:

To know what your partner wants from their relationship with your family, especially with your parents.

Why it's Important:

Relationships with in-laws can have a big effect on how well a couple gets along, so it is important to talk about this early on.

Possible Answers:

- "I'd like to have a friendly and respectful relationship with my in-laws."

- "I believe in-laws can become like a second set of parents, so I'd love to build a strong relationship with them."

Follow-Up Questions:

- Have you had any difficult experiences with in-laws in the past? How did you handle it?

- What steps would you take to build a positive relationship with my family?

On a Lighter Note:

"So, do you picture yourself having matching holiday sweaters with my parents, or will a polite nod at family gatherings do?"

Positive and Negative Aspects:

Positive: Having clear expectations can help stop misunderstandings and fights in the future.

Negative: If people's expectations are not the same, it can cause tension and fights.

Self-Reflection:

Think about how you and your parents get along and how you would like your partner to fit into that.

Practical Guidance:

Talk about how you feel, what you need, or what you value in your relationship with your in-laws. Focus on respect, connection, boundaries, or expectations to figure out what shapes, helps, or hurts this relationship.

Think about how you'll deal with, help, and grow your relationship with your in-laws. Think about ways to build mutual respect, understanding, connection, or boundaries in these relationships.

Set up regular "family meetings" or talks to make sure that you and your partner agree on how your in-laws fit into your life.

Holistic Viewpoints:

Getting to know your in-laws is a process with many parts that are affected by cultural, social, and personal factors. For people who identify as LGBTQ+, there may be problems with acceptance or understanding in the family, for example. These problems are hard to solve and require sensitivity, empathy, and an open mind. Respecting different family structures and ways of talking is very important. When it comes to setting limits or making close connections, the key is to be aware of each person's preferences and how each family unit works.

For Long-term Relationships:

When two people have been together for a long time, their interactions with their in-laws can change and grow. This could mean getting used to new roles in the family, dealing with conflicts, or making deeper connections. For these changes to go smoothly, partners must talk to each other regularly and honestly. Understanding what each other wants, how they feel, and how comfortable they are with the in-laws helps everyone work together. It helps get decisions and responses in sync, which makes family gatherings more fun and makes relationships with in-laws more satisfying.

Expert Insight:

Studies, like the one by Serewicz, Hosmer, Ballard, and Griffin[2], show that having good relationships with your in-laws is an important part of being happy in your marriage. To have good relationships with in-laws, it's important to find a balance between respect, assertiveness, and flexibility. Customizing communication strategies to the way your family works and being honest with your partner about how you feel and what you want sets the stage for more harmonious relationships.

---

2. Serewicz, M. C. M., Hosmer, R., Ballard, R. L., & Griffin, R. A. (2012). Disclosure from In-laws and the Quality of In-law and Marital Relationships.

Question #34:

How much involvement do you think your parents should have in our lives?

Purpose:

To understand how much your partner's parents are involved in your life together from your partner's point of view.

Why it's Important:

The level of parental involvement can affect how independent a couple is, how they make decisions, and how their relationship works as a whole.

Possible Answers:

- "I value my parents' input, but I believe decisions should be made by us."

- "While I love my parents, I think it's important for us to lead our own lives."

Follow-Up Questions:

- How do you see us balancing our time between our families?

- How would you handle it if you felt my parents were becoming too involved in our lives?

On a Lighter Note:

"Do you envision your parents as honorary members of our household or more like guest stars in the sitcom of our life?"

Positive and Negative Aspects:

Positive: Talking about this makes sure that everyone understands and stops future fights.

Negative: If expectations aren't aligned, it could lead to tension between the couple and their parents.

Self-Reflection:

Think about your own limits when it comes to your parents. Are there specific areas where you prefer minimal interference?

Practical Guidance:

Talk about how you feel, what you need, or what you believe about parental involvement. Focusing on connection, boundaries, autonomy, or well-being can help you figure out what drives, shapes, or tests this part of your life.

Think about how you will handle, help, or balance the involvement of your parents in your relationship. Think about ways to encourage mutual respect, understanding, connection, or autonomy when it comes to how parents are involved.

Exercise: Talk about and write down specific limits and expectations for parental involvement. This will help you and your partner figure out how to handle this part of your lives.

Holistic Viewpoints:

The role of parents in a couple's life changes a lot depending on their culture, society, and personal situation. In some cultures, parents play a big role, helping kids make decisions and giving them constant support. On the other hand, there are times when a couple may want more freedom. To understand these differences, you need to be culturally sensitive and willing to learn about and respect the values and traditions that lie beneath them. Open communication about expectations, values, and limits helps people come to an agreement that works for both of them, taking into account both personal preferences and cultural norms

For Long-term Relationships:

As relationships grow and life stages change, the type and amount of parental involvement may change. The dynamics can change when children come along, when parents get older, or when something important happens. Talking about parental involvement again at different points in a person's life helps keep a balance that makes sense in the current situation. Continuous conversation helps couples adjust and makes sure that both partners are happy with the level of parental involvement in their lives, whether that means accepting more help or keeping the same boundaries.

Expert Insight:

Studies like the one done by Fingerman et al.[3] show how important it is to find a healthy balance between being independent and staying close to your parents. Finding this balance can help people be happier in their relationships and grow as people. This complicated relationship is shaped by how often you talk to your parents, how clear your boundaries are, and how much you respect each other. The advice from professionals shows how important it is to recognize and value the good things about parental involvement while also recognizing the importance of autonomy and individual growth within the partnership.

---

3. Fingerman KL, et al. (2012). Helicopter Parents and Landing Pad Kids: Intense Parental Support of Grown Children.

CHAPTER SEVEN

FRIENDS

CULTIVATING SUPPORTIVE FRIENDSHIPS WITHIN AND OUTSIDE THE RELATIONSHIP

Question #35:

How important are your friendships to you?

Purpose:

This question is meant to help you figure out how your partner feels about friendships and what role they play in their life. This can give you clues about their social life, support system, and values.

Why It's Important:

Understanding the value someone places on friendships can give insight into their social needs and priorities.

Possible Answers:

- "I value my friendships very much. They offer support and companionship."

- "I value my friendships, but I also like spending time by myself or with my partner."

Follow-up Questions:

- How do you balance time between friends and your significant other?

- How do your friends influence your life and decisions?

- Do you maintain long-term friendships?

On a Lighter Note:

"If they call themselves the "Michael Scott" of their office, expect uncomfortable jokes and a never-ending supply of "that's what she said." At least every day will seem like an episode of "The Office," and who wouldn't want to be part of that eccentric family?"

Positive and Negative Aspects:

Positive: If you know how much your partner values their friendships, you can learn about their social needs and how they keep in touch with people.

Negative: Different ideas about what friends are for in life can sometimes cause misunderstandings or fights.

Self-Reflection:

Think about the friends you have and how important they are to you. How might this impact your potential relationship?

Practical Guidance:

Talk about how your friends have changed your life and helped you grow as a person. How do your friends affect your daily life, your emotional health, and your growth as a person? How do you take care of and keep these relationships going?

Find out how you and your partner balance your friendships with your other responsibilities and relationships, including your romantic one. How do you plan to keep putting your friends first and investing in them once you're engaged?

Talk about any worries or limits that might need to be set in your relationship about your friendships. How will you support and respect each other's friendships while also keeping your partnership's promises and priorities?

Holistic Viewpoints:

Friendships and how important they are to different people can vary a lot, depending on their needs, preferences, and situations in life. Some people have a lot of friends and get energy and happiness from being around a lot of people. Others might find happiness in just a few close, intimate friendships or even mostly in relationships with family or a significant other. Also, some people can meet their social needs by making online friends through online communities. Recognizing these differences is important for understanding and respecting the different ways people make friends and connect with each other.

For Long-term Relationships:

Friendships can grow and change over time in the context of a long-term relationship. Changes in interests, life stages, or personal growth can cause friendships to grow, change, or end. This can also lead to the creation of new friendships. It's important for people in a relationship to talk openly about these changes and figure out how they might affect the relationship. Some people might think it's important for their own well-being to keep their own friendships going, while others might care more about the shared friendships or the partnership itself. Finding a balance that meets both people's needs can help make a relationship more fulfilling and peaceful.

Expert Insight:

Several studies have looked at how important friends are in addition to romantic relationships. In his book "Buddy System: Understanding Male Friendships,"[1] Dr. Geoffrey Greif, a professor at the University of Maryland School of Social Work, talks about how important friendships are. He says that friendships give support and growth in ways that a romantic relationship might not. This shows how important it is to value and take care of friendships as well as romantic relationships since they each play different roles in a person's social and emotional health.

---

1. Greif, Geoffrey L. "Buddy System: Understanding Male Friendships." Oxford University Press, 2008

Question #36:

How do you feel about having friends of different genders? Do you have any boundaries regarding these friendships?

Purpose:

This question is meant to find out how comfortable and open-minded your partner is with you having friends of different genders. It also gives you an idea of how your partner feels about trust, jealousy, and what is considered appropriate behavior in friendships.

Why It's Important:

This question addresses trust and boundaries within a relationship, fostering a climate of understanding and respect.

Possible Answers:

- "I have no problem making friends with people of any gender. I believe in trust and openness."

- "I do have friends of different genders, but I also think there should be some limits to respect my relationship."

Follow-up Questions:

- Have your friendships with people of different genders ever created issues in your past relationships?

- What specific boundaries do you think should exist?

- How would you react if I had close friends of a different gender?

On a Lighter Note:

If they state that having friends of different genders is like having the ultimate decoder ring for understanding the opposite sex, well, you might just have a communication superhero on your hands!

Positive and Negative Aspects:

Positive: Getting to know each other's comfort zones and limits can help prevent misunderstandings and build trust.

Negative: Keep in mind that it is important to talk about and deal with feelings of restriction or mistrust when boundaries are set.

Self-Reflection:

Reflect on your own comfort levels and boundaries with having friends of different genders. Are you on the same page as your partner?

Practical Guidance:

Talk about what it's like to have friends of different genders and what you think about it. How have these friendships changed you and what you care about? Why do you think they are important or meaningful?

Find out if there are any worries, fears, or misunderstandings about friendships between people of different genders. How have these played out in past relationships, and how might you deal with them in this one?

Talk about any rules or agreements you might want to set for these friendships to help build trust and understanding between you. How will you talk to each other and get around these differences?

Remember that there is no one answer to this question that works for everyone. It's about finding a shared understanding that fits both of your values, experiences, and needs, and being willing to keep talking and growing in this area.

Holistic Viewpoints:

In a diverse society where friendships often cross gender lines, it's important to know and respect that people of different genders can and do have platonic relationships. It's just as important to understand and care about friends who don't fit into traditional gender roles. These friendships aren't just based on being the same gender; they're also based on having similar interests, values, and experiences, which helps bring people together. So, judging or limiting friendships based only on gender can stop people from growing as people and cause them to miss out on chances to have more meaningful social interactions. Also, keep in mind that in some religions, having friends of the opposite gender while being engaged or married can be frowned upon.

For Long-term Relationships:

In long-term relationships, it's often hard to find a good balance between staying friends with each other and making the relationship stronger. Over time, people can make new friends and old ones can change or end. Having friends of different genders can make this mix more interesting. It is important to talk openly and honestly about comfort levels, expectations, and limits in these friendships. It's not just about making rules; it's also about understanding how each other feels, finding things you have in common, and growing as a group in a way that respects each person's independence and works with them.

Expert Insight:

Experts like Dr. Suzanne Degges-White[2] and studies like those in the Journal of Social and Personal Relationships can help you figure out how to be friends with people of different

---

2. https://www.psychologytoday.com/us/blog/lifetime-connections/202111/the-7-types-friends-and-which-is-most-essential-our-happiness

genders while you're in a relationship. Dr. Degges-White says that it's healthy and normal for people to have friends of different genders. But it's important to be honest and open about these friendships. When people talk to each other often and clearly, they are more likely to trust each other, avoid misunderstandings, and feel less jealous. Research also shows that each couple needs to set their own limits because what works for one couple might not work for another. So, you have to talk to each other often and be willing to adjust to each other's changing needs and feelings. Couples can keep a healthy balance between their friendships and romantic relationships if they use these tips.

Question #37:

How do you see my friends fitting into our lives as a couple?

Purpose:

This question will help you figure out how your partner thinks your friendships fit into your life together. It can show how open they are, how flexible they are, and how much they value friendships outside of their relationship.

Why It's Important:

This question can reveal how your partner views the balance between couple time and socializing, important for lifestyle compatibility.

Possible Answers:

- "I think of them as a part of our family that has grown. I would love to meet them and talk with them about our lives."

- "I believe in balance. Even though it is important to hang out with friends, we also need time to ourselves."

Follow-up Questions:

- How would you feel about regular gatherings with my friends?

- Are there any concerns you have about my friends?

- How comfortable are you with me spending time alone with my friends?

On a Lighter Note:

If they say, "I see your friends as future partners-in-crime for our weekend barbecues and game nights!", expect some lively social gatherings ahead!

Positive and Negative Aspects:

Positive: When you value and include each other's friendships, you can make your shared life better.

Negative: You should also make sure your partner is comfortable and that your friends do not get in the way of your alone time.

Self-Reflection:

Think about what you want your partner's friends to do in your life together. Do you and your partner share similar views?

Practical Guidance:

Talk about how you feel, what you expect, and what you hope will happen with your partner's friends in your life together. What role do you think they play in social activities, support systems, or experiences that people share?

Look into any worries or limits that might need to be talked about in terms of friendships. How will you deal with different levels of comfort or expectations when it comes to letting friends into your lives?

Talk about how you'll talk about your friends and make decisions about them, especially if they affect your time, priorities, and other commitments as a couple. How will you support and respect each other's friendships while also growing your own?

Holistic Viewpoints:

Do not forget to respect and acknowledge the different people you know. Be open-minded, accepting, and friendly to people who come from different cultures, orientations, or walks of life.

For Long-term Relationships:

As life changes and friendships evolve, keep the conversation about the role of friends in your shared life ongoing.

Expert Insight - Attachment Styles:

Secure Attachment Style: People who have this style are usually sure of themselves and don't mind if their partner has close friends. Most of the time, they know how important it is to keep their own friendships even though they are in a relationship. They may want to get to know your friends and include them in social activities they do with you, but they will also tell you to spend time with your friends on your own.

Anxious Attachment Style: People with this style may worry or feel uneasy about how your friends will fit into your life as a couple. They might be afraid that spending time with your friends will take time away from the relationship, or they might be afraid of fights or disagreements. But they may also show a strong desire to be a part of your friendships and social activities, hoping that this will help them get closer to you.

Avoidant Attachment Style: People with this style may stress how important it is to keep their own social circles and independence. They might not want to mix their social lives much and would rather keep their friendships separate. They might be glad that you have friends of your own, but they might not be as interested in doing things with you and your friends as a group.

Disorganized Attachment Style: People with this style may have mixed feelings about the role of friends in their lives. Sometimes they may want to hang out with your friends, and sometimes they may want to stay away. It may be hard to guess how they will act because it will depend on how they are feeling at the time.

Question #38:

What qualities do you value most in your friends?

Purpose:

This question can tell you about your partner's personality and what they might value in a romantic relationship based on what they value in their social circle.

Why it's Important:

If you know what your partner likes in their friends, you can learn more about their social preferences and maybe figure out what they may be looking for in you.

Possible Answers:

- "I value honesty, reliability, and a sense of humor in my friends."

- "Kindness, understanding, and a shared interest are important to me in friendships."

Follow-Up Questions:

- How do these qualities reflect your values or ideals?

- Can you share an example of how these qualities have played out in your friendships?

On a Lighter Note:

"As long as my friends share my love for cheesy 90s music and bad dad jokes, we're good!"

Positive and Negative Aspects:

Positive: If your partner values honesty, loyalty, and kindness in their friends, it is likely that they also value these qualities in a relationship.

Negative: It could be worrying if the things they value most are shallow or could hurt them (like partying too much or talking too much).

Self-Reflection:

Think about what you look for in your friends. Do they match the values of your partner? What do they say about what you want from a romantic partner?

Practical Guidance:

Knowing what you look for in a friend can help you understand each other's social life and values.

Talk about what you like about your friends and why. Discuss how these may or may not be different from what you value in your relationship.

Exercise: Each pair makes a "friendship collage" that shows what they like best about their friends. Talk about how these values could be applied to your own relationship.

Holistic Viewpoints:

Different people look for different things in the friends they have. Different things can give rise to these preferences.

Cultures have their own norms and values, which can have a big effect on what a person wants in a friend. For example, some cultures may put a lot of value on loyalty and close relationships, while others may stress individuality and freedom.

Personal Values: Morality, ethics, and personality, which are all personal values, also play a role. When you know how these values affect a person's friendships, you can learn more about who they are.

For Long-term Relationships:

In a long-term friendship, it's important to understand and agree with each other's friendship values.

Values that change: As people grow and change, so may the things they value in their friendships. Regular talks about this topic can keep people on the same page and help them understand each other better.

Shared Values: People who have been together for a long time often have the same friends. When people are friends, it can be helpful to know what each other cares about.

Expert Insight – Attachment Styles:

People who know a lot about psychology and relationships talk about how important friendships are.

Self-Reflection: As was already said, friends can show different parts of a person's personality. When you know what your partner looks for in friends, you can learn more about who they are.

Friendships outside of a romantic relationship can have a positive or negative effect on the relationship itself. Having the same ideas about what makes a good friend makes for a supportive environment.

Attachment styles: A person's attachment style has a big effect on how they treat their friends.

Secure Attachment Style: People with secure attachment tend to value trust, empathy, and emotional connections that are both strong and stable. They might try to find friends who are like them in these ways.

Anxious Attachment Style: People with this type of attachment may need constant reassurance and connection, and they may value friends who are always available and responsive.

Avoidant Attachment Style: People with this style may want less emotional closeness in their friendships and value independence and being able to do things on their own.

Disorganized Attachment Style: People with this style of attachment may have different needs and wants in their friendships, like wanting to be close or being afraid of being close. Getting this can lead to more understanding and help.

Chapter Eight

Communication

The Art of Open Dialogue and Emotional Connection

Question #39:

Are you comfortable with expressing your feelings and concerns?

Purpose:

The point of this question is to find out how comfortable your partner is with showing how they feel and how they talk. It shows how open they are, how vulnerable they are, and how emotionally smart they are.

Why It's Important:

Open emotional communication is key to understanding and supporting each other. This question encourages emotional honesty.

Possible Answers:

- "Yes, I am usually fine talking about how I feel."

- "It is hard for me, but I am trying to get better at it."

- "I usually show how I feel through what I do instead of what I say."

Follow-up Questions:

- What makes you feel safe or unsafe when expressing your feelings? What makes you feel safe or unsafe when sharing your feelings?

- Can you share an example of a time when you felt comfortable or uncomfortable sharing your feelings? Can you give an example of a time when it was easy or hard for you to talk about how you felt?

- How do you want me to respond when you share your feelings?

On a Lighter Note:

If they use songs from musical theater to show how they feel, you are in for an emotional roller coaster and some great dance performances.

Positive and Negative Aspects:

Positive: Being able to talk about your feelings can help you get closer to people and solve problems better.

Negative: Not being able to say how you feel could be a sign of past hurts or problems communicating.

Self-Reflection:

What do you think about letting your feelings show? What situations or actions make you feel safe or unsafe when you talk about how you feel?

Practical Guidance:

Talk about how comfortable you are with expressing your feelings and worries. What makes it simple or hard? Is it harder to talk about certain feelings or subjects?

Find out how each of you likes to talk about how you feel. Need time to think before you speak? Do you like to write down your thoughts first, or do you like to talk about things as they come up?

Talk about what you need from each other when you tell each other how you feel or what worries you. This could mean listening without judging, asking open-ended questions, or giving reassurance and support.

Consider making your relationship a "safe space" where both of you feel free to talk about anything. This could mean setting aside regular time to check in with each other, agreeing on clear rules for how to talk to each other, or making rituals that make you feel closer emotionally.

Being able to talk about your feelings and worries means not only telling your partner what's going on inside you but also making it safe for them to do the same.

Holistic Viewpoints:

Culture, gender stereotypes, and one's own life can all have a big impact on how comfortable someone is with expressing their feelings. For example, in some cultures, showing emotions out in the open might not be the norm, or men might be discouraged by social norms from showing certain emotions. Know and respect these things, and make sure that your relationship is a safe place where you can be yourself.

For Long-term Relationships:

In a long-term relationship, the ease with which you can talk about your feelings and worries is not a constant. Instead, it is a part of the relationship that is always changing and needs attention, care, and sometimes a readjustment. Partners may find that their ability to talk about their feelings changes as their situations, stresses, and even successes change. To make sure that both partners continue to feel safe and understood, it's important to create an environment where emotional openness is not only accepted but celebrated. This could mean checking in with each other often, being aware of each other's emotional needs, and developing a shared language that goes beyond words. And when problems come up, knowing the value of professional help is not a sign of weakness but of strength, because it shows a commitment to not just keep the emotional connection going but to make it stronger.

Self-Reflection:

A person's attachment style affects how well they can talk about their feelings and worries. Here is how each style may approach this:

Secure Attachment Style: People who have a secure attachment style find it easy to talk about how they feel and what worries them. They are comfortable being emotionally close to each other and believe that their partner will respond with understanding and care. They also understand the importance of sharing emotions for maintaining a healthy and balanced relationship.

Anxious Attachment Style: People with this attachment style often have strong feelings and a strong desire to show them. But they may be afraid that if they talk about their feelings or worries, they will be rejected or abandoned. This fear can make them share too much and become too dependent on their partner for emotional support, or it can make them hide their feelings to avoid a fight.

Avoidant Attachment Style: People with this style may find it hard to talk about how they feel and what worries them. They like being on their own and may think that showing emotions is a sign of weakness or a threat to their freedom. This style often makes them emotionally distant and keeps them from sharing their feelings with their partner, which can make it hard to talk to each other and get close emotionally.

Disorganized Attachment Style: People with a disorganized attachment style may not be able to express their feelings and worries in a predictable way. They may go from being too emotional to not showing any emotion at all. This is because they both want emotional intimacy and are afraid of it at the same time.

Expert Insight:

Psychologists, therapists, and relationship experts often talk about how important it is to show how you feel in a relationship. It's more than just a way to say what's on our minds; it's a way to get closer, build trust, and really connect with someone. Experts say that it's just as important to understand and accept each other's emotional styles as it is to express ourselves. Some people's feelings may come easily, while others may need to be pushed to feel them. The journey is not just about talking, but also about listening, understanding, and feeling what someone else feels. Emotional expression is a shared dance that can lead to lasting intimacy and connection if done with openness, respect, and a willingness to explore not only the emotions themselves but also what lies beneath them. It's about making a place where feelings can be shared and valued, which can lead to a richer, more meaningful relationship.

Question #40:

How often do you think we should check in with each other emotionally?

Purpose:

This question gives you an idea of how your partner feels about maintaining and understanding emotions. It tells how often people should talk about how they feel.

Why It's Important:

Regular emotional check-ins can help keep communication lines open and support emotional health within the relationship.

Possible Answers:

- "Daily, like taking vitamins for the relationship."

- "Every week, when it is time for us to talk heart-to-heart."

Follow-up Questions:

- What does an emotional check-in look like to you?

- How comfortable are you in initiating these check-ins?

On a Lighter Note:

"And remember, this is not a dental check-up; no drills involved, promise!"

Positive and Negative Aspects:

Positive: Checking in on each other's feelings on a regular basis can strengthen relationships and keep people from getting confused.

Negative: But if you force them too often, it might feel intrusive or pointless to some.

Self-Reflection:

Think about what your emotional needs are and how often you would like to check in. Can you live up to your partner's hopes?

Practical Guidance:

Talk about what you want, what you need, or what you value during regular emotional check-ins. Focusing on time, attention, openness, or shared rituals can help you figure out what helps or hurts meaningful emotional connections for each of you.

Explore how you will include, balance, or put emotional check-ins at regular intervals in your relationship. Think about ways to encourage emotional engagement that is genuine, attentive, and enriching. What habits, rituals, or ways of thinking might people share?

Holistic Viewpoints:

Emotionally checking in is an important part of a healthy relationship, but the "right" number of times to do this will vary a lot from couple to couple.

Individual Needs: Some people might want to talk about their feelings often, even every day, while others might find that too much or not necessary. It's important to understand the needs of each partner and find a balance that works for both.

Considerations for neurodiversity: If one or both partners are neurodiverse, traditional emotional check-ins might not be the best way to communicate. It might be better to find other ways to talk about feelings and emotional well-being.

Cultural Factors: Different cultures have different rules about how to show how you feel. Some people may be used to talking about their feelings often and openly, while others may be more reserved. It is important to understand and respect these cultural differences.

Quality Over Quantity: The focus shouldn't just be on how often to check in, but also on how meaningful and real those checks-in are. A heartfelt conversation once a week might be more valuable than a routine question every day.

For Long-term Relationships:

Emotional check-ins can be even more complicated for people who have been together for a long time.

Routine can lead to problems: Long-term relationships can become boring, and important emotional communication can be missed. Setting aside time on purpose for deep conversations can help people stay emotionally connected.

Changing with Life Stages: As people go through different stages of life, their emotional needs and ways of talking to each other may change. To keep the emotional bond strong, it's important to notice these changes and adjust to them.

Creating a Customized Approach: Couples who have been together for a long time often come up with their own ways to talk to each other that fit the way their relationship works. By going over and changing these patterns often, you can make sure they continue to meet the emotional needs of both partners.

Expert Insight – Attachment Styles:

Secure Attachment Style: People with a secure attachment style usually have a balanced view when it comes to checking in emotionally with their partner. They know it's important to check in with each other often about how they're feeling, but they also give each other their space. They will probably suggest a few dates that will bring you closer together and build trust without being too much.

Anxious Attachment Style: People with this style might feel like they need to check in on their partner's feelings more often than their partner is comfortable with. They might think that if they're reassured, the relationship is usually safe.

Avoidant Attachment Style: People with this style may not feel the need for frequent emotional check-ins because they value their independence and may find such conversations too intrusive or clingy. They might want to talk less about how they feel.

Disorganized Attachment Style: For people with a disorganized attachment style, how often they check in on how they're feeling depends on how they're feeling. There may be times when they want emotional check-ins often, and other times when they want to be alone and less connected.

Question #41:

What are your emotional needs?

Purpose:

To figure out what your partner needs emotionally, how they like to have these needs met, and how you can better understand their emotional landscape.

Why it's Important:

Being aware of each other's emotional needs can strengthen your emotional connection and help you learn more about each other, which will improve the quality of your relationship.

Possible Answers:

- "I need regular reassurances of love and commitment, and open, honest communication about feelings."

- "I value understanding, patience, and a space to express my feelings without judgment."

Follow-Up Questions:

- How can I best fulfill these emotional needs?

- How do you communicate when your emotional needs aren't being met?

On a Lighter Note:

"I need to feel loved, appreciated, and on some days, I just need someone to laugh with me at my ridiculous puns. Get ready!"

Positive and Negative Aspects:

Positive: Being aware of and meeting each other's emotional needs can make the relationship stronger and make both people happier.

Negative: If you do not understand or do not care about these needs, it could make you feel neglected or unhappy.

Self-Reflection:

Think about your own emotional needs and how they match or differ from those of your partner.

Practical Guidance:

Talk about how you feel, what you need, what you value, or what you've learned about emotional needs. Focus on connection, understanding, validation, or support to figure out what helps, hurts, or challenges your emotional health.

Find out how you will handle each other's emotional needs, support each other, or meet each other's needs. Think about ways to help your relationship have more empathy, validation, responsiveness, or shared growth.

Use an "emotional needs inventory" to talk about and figure out how to meet each partner's most important needs in the relationship.

Holistic Viewpoints:

Emotional needs are complex and come from many different parts of a person's life, such as their culture, upbringing, past relationships, and personal values. Understanding these needs is not a one-size-fits-all job, because what is important to one person may not be important to another. In this complicated world, it's important to have an open mind, empathy, and nonjudgmental curiosity. Respect and trust are built on a foundation of acceptance of the unique emotional needs of each person.

For Long-term Relationships:

Emotional needs are complex and come from many parts of a person's life, such as culture, upbringing, past relationships, and personal values. Understanding these needs is not a one-size-fits-all job, because what is important to one person might not be important to another. To get around in this complicated world, you need to have an open mind, empathy, and nonjudgmental curiosity. Respect and trust are built on a foundation of understanding that each person's emotional needs are unique.

Expert Insight – Attachment Styles:

Secure Attachment Style: People who have a secure attachment style are usually okay with both closeness and being on their own. They usually have a good opinion of themselves and others, which helps them keep their emotional needs in check and communicate well with others.

Anxious Attachment Style: People with this style of attachment often worry about being rejected or left alone, and they may need reassurance and closeness more than others. They may try to get approval from their partner all the time, which can make them seem needy or clingy.

Avoidant Attachment Style: This style is marked by a focus on self-sufficiency, often at the expense of intimacy. People with dismissive-avoidant attachment may have trouble expressing their emotional needs and may keep others at a distance to keep their independence.

Disorganized Attachment Style: People with this style of attachment may want to be close to others but also want to be on their own. They may have trouble trusting people and be afraid of getting too close to them. This can lead to a complicated mix of emotional needs.

Question #42:

How can I best support you when you're stressed or upset?

Purpose:

To learn the best ways to help your partner when they are stressed or upset, which will help them understand and care for you.

Why it's Important:

Knowing how to help each other through hard times can make a relationship much stronger and healthier overall.

Possible Answers:

- "Sometimes I just need a listening ear, other times, I might need some space to process my feelings."

- "Offering comfort, reassurance, and a distraction from what's causing the stress always helps."

Follow-Up Questions:

- What doesn't help when you're stressed or upset?

- Can you tell me about a time when someone supported you in a way that was particularly helpful?

On a Lighter Note:

"Are you a 'chocolate and rom-com' kind of person or a 'let's punch pillows until we feel better' one?"

Positive and Negative Aspects:

Positive: By asking this question, you show your partner that you want to be there for them and that you care about them.

Negative: Not understanding someone or not giving them the help they need can make them feel alone or frustrated.

Self-Reflection:

Think about how you usually need help when you are upset and if your partner's favorite ways to get help are the same as yours.

Practical Guidance:

Talk about how you like to get help when you're stressed or upset, what you need, or what you've done in the past. Focus on empathy, understanding, validation, or comfort to figure out what helps, hurts, or makes you feel good about yourself.

Think about how you will get through hard times together, how you will help each other, and how you will get help from each other. What might be involved in terms of shared empathy, responsiveness, trust, or understanding?

Exercise: Make a "stress-support plan" that lists each partner's preferred ways to be helped and their most common stress triggers.

Holistic Viewpoints:

To know how to help a partner when they are stressed, you have to be aware of how different people's needs are based on their cultural backgrounds, personal experiences, and personal preferences. What makes one person feel better might not help another. Respectful questioning, active listening, and the ability to change are all very important.

By accepting that your partner's feelings are different from your own, you can build a connection that is caring and responsive.

For Long-term Relationships:

In long-term relationships, people's needs for support may change over time as their lives change, they grow emotionally, or the way the relationship works changes. You can make sure your support fits your partner's current needs by talking to them often, showing empathy, and paying attention to small signs. Building a shared understanding of what comfort and reassurance look like in different situations helps people get closer and trust each other more.

Expert Insight – Attachment Styles:

Secure Attachment Style: People who have a secure attachment style are usually clear about what they need and like a balanced response that acknowledges their feelings without making them feel smothered. They value empathy, understanding, and a way of doing things that promotes both connection and independence.

Anxious Attachment Style: People with this style may be more sensitive to stress and look for reassurance more often. They often benefit from constant affirmation, loving presence, and a clear commitment to their well-being. It can be especially comforting to show that you understand and are there for them emotionally.

Avoidant Attachment Style: People with this style often pull away when they are stressed because they value independence and being able to take care of themselves. Instead of giving them emotional support right away, it might be more helpful to respect their need for space and reassure them that they can handle the situation. Most of the time, the right balance is reached when someone is available but not too pushy.

Disorganized Attachment Style: When a person's attachment isn't well-organized, their need for support can be complicated and even contradictory. These people might want to be close and far away at the same time. The key may be to take a gentle approach that acknowledges this tension and offers support without putting too much pressure on the person. This emotional terrain is hard to get through without clear communication and patience.

Question #43:

How do your personality traits complement or contrast with mine, and how can we leverage that for a successful relationship?

Purpose:

This question is meant to find out how your partner sees the compatibility of your individual personality traits and how they might change the way your relationship works.

Why it's Important:

Understanding your individual traits and how they interact with each other can help you see how you work as a team, point out potential problems, and show you how to use your strengths to make your partnership stronger.

Possible Answers:

- "Our differences could bring balance and broaden our perspectives, while similarities could strengthen our bond."

- "While I'm more introverted and you're outgoing, we can learn from each other and have a well-rounded social life."

Follow-Up Questions:

- What personality traits do you value in a partner?

- Can you give examples of how our personality traits have interacted in our relationship so far?

On a Lighter Note:

"I think your introverted nature and my extroverted one create a great balance. You help me slow down and enjoy quiet moments, while I push you to explore social scenarios. Together, we might just create the perfect party – one where we both actually want to be there!"

Positive and Negative Aspects:

Positive: Being aware of traits that go together can help you appreciate and respect each other while being aware of traits that go against each other can help you prepare for potential conflicts and come up with ways to handle them.

Negative: This conversation could bring up disagreements or things that people think are wrong, which could be hard to deal with.

Self-Reflection:

Think about your personality and how it might go with or against your partner's. Think about times when your qualities helped or got in the way of the relationship.

Practical Guidance:

Pay close attention to what your partner has to say and be open to what they say. Use this as a chance to find out more about each other and come up with ways to help each other's unique qualities.

Holistic Viewpoints:

People can have very different personality traits, and these differences can be caused by things like culture, upbringing, and life experiences. Here's how to think about these things:

Understanding Differences: Being aware that different backgrounds can lead to different personality traits helps people be more accepting and empathetic.

Growth through Diversity: When used well, contrasting personality traits can help a person grow and learn. This can help people connect and understand each other better.

For Long-term Relationships:

In a long-term relationship, it's important to keep learning about how personalities work:

Personalities that change: As both people grow and change, personality traits may also change. By talking about these changes and thinking about them often, you can keep the relationship strong.

Balancing Strengths and Weaknesses: People who have been together for a long time can learn to use each other's strengths and help each other with their weaknesses. This creates a synergistic relationship.

Expert Insight:

Psychological insights help us understand and use personality traits in a relationship in a deeper way:

Personality assessments: Tools like the Myers-Briggs Type Indicator (MBTI) or the Big Five Personality Traits can help you learn about your partner's personality and give you a place to start talking and getting to know them.

Styles of Communication: Knowing how each partner communicates based on their personality traits can improve how well they talk to each other.

Conflict Resolution: Knowing how each partner usually reacts to a disagreement based on their personality traits can help you come up with better ways to solve conflicts.

Question #44:

Have you experienced any significant emotional or psychological traumas in your life? How have they affected you?

Purpose:

The goal is to find out if your partner has been through any major emotional or psychological traumas and how they have affected them as a person.

Why it's important:

Talking about past traumas can help you understand each other's behaviors, reactions, fears, and needs better. It makes people more compassionate and empathetic, helps them figure out what sets them off, and can lead to a more supportive and understanding relationship.

Possible Answers:

- "I've had some hard times that affected me, but I've learned and grown from them."

- "I've been through some hard things that I'm still working through, and I might need your help sometimes."

Follow-up Questions:

- Would it be okay for you to talk about what happened?

- What do you need from me in terms of support or understanding about these things?

- Have you gone to a professional for help? How did that go?

Positive and Negative Aspects:

Positive: It makes people more open, strengthens relationships, and helps people understand and help each other.

Negative: It could be painful or upsetting, so it's important to talk about it carefully.

Self-Reflection:

What about your own traumas? How do you feel about sharing them? What kind of help might you need?

Practical Guidance:

Find a safe, private place to talk about this.

Be kind, patient, and empathetic.

Be aware that this conversation could be painful or upsetting, and you may need to talk to someone else or get help from a professional.

Holistic Viewpoints:

Exploring traumas isn't just about learning about the past; it's also about how these events affect the relationship in the present. It's a chance to get closer through understanding and help.

For Long-term Relationships:

Talking about this topic all the time can lead to support that changes as both people grow and change. It can build trust and make people feel closer to each other.

Expert Insight – Attachment Styles:

Secure Attachment Style: Likely to approach this topic with care, offering support and understanding.

Anxious Attachment Style: May be afraid of being judged or being left alone, and needs gentle reassurance.

Avoidant Attachment Style: They might be reluctant to talk about feelings, so they need to be gently pushed.

Disorganized Attachment Style: This conversation could be hard and need to be handled carefully.

Understanding each other's traumas and how they've changed you as people can help you feel closer, have more empathy for each other, and be more supportive in a relationship. It's a sensitive topic that needs kindness, patience, and maybe even help from a professional, but it can also be a powerful way for everyone to learn more about each other and grow in understanding and compassion.

Question #45:

Are there any specific triggers or situations that I should be aware of to ensure that I'm considerate of your past experiences?

Purpose:

The goal is to find out if your partner has any specific triggers or situations that make them feel bad because of things that happened in the past. This will help you be more understanding and helpful in the relationship.

Why it's Important:

Knowing a partner's triggers can help you avoid accidentally hurting or upsetting them, improve communication, and create a nurturing environment.

Possible Answers:

- "I'm sensitive to loud noises because of something that happened in the past. If you know we'll be somewhere noisy, it would be helpful to let me know."

- "I'm afraid of being left alone, so it's hard for me when plans change quickly."

Follow-up Questions:

- What can I do if I do something by accident that makes something happen for you?

- How can we work together to keep these things from making our relationship worse?

Positive and Negative Aspects:

Positive: It makes the relationship more caring, respectful, and supportive.

Negative: It might be hard or emotional to talk to them.

Self-reflection:

Do you have any triggers or sensitivities that your partner needs to be aware of and careful around?

Practical Guidance:

Go into this conversation with an open mind and a desire to understand.

Remind them that the goal is to help each other out more.

Holistic Viewpoints:

Learning about triggers isn't just about avoiding them; it's also about figuring out how to deal with them as a group. This makes it easier for people to trust and care about each other.

For Long-Term Relationships:

This conversation can go on for a long time, because understanding and dealing with triggers may change over time and as the relationship grows.

Expert Insight:

Different people have different ways of communicating. Some people may find it easy to talk about triggers, while others may need more time and reassurance. Change how you act based on how comfortable your partner is.

One important part of emotional intelligence in a relationship is being aware of each other's triggers. It takes open communication, understanding, and a willingness to help each other through memories or experiences that could be painful. This conversation sets the stage for a caring and supportive relationship in which both people feel heard and cared for.

Question #46:

How do you cope with difficult emotions or triggers that might stem from your past traumas?

Purpose:

The goal is to learn how your partner deals with hard feelings or triggers related to past traumas. This will help you understand and support their ways of coping.

Why it's Important:

Knowing how your partner deals with triggers or hard feelings can help you understand them and help them in the way they need. This is very important for making the relationship feel safe and supportive.

Possible Answers:

- "Most of the time, I need some time alone to figure out how I feel."

- "It helps me to talk about how I'm feeling with a close friend or a therapist."

- "When I need to calm down, I do certain things, like working out or meditating."

Follow-up Questions:

- Is there anything, in particular, you'd like me to do or not do when you're having these feelings or experiencing these triggers?

- Would you like me to support you or help you with these ways to deal with stress?

Positive and Negative Aspects:

Positive: It helps them understand each other better and gives them more support.

Negative: This conversation might make you think of or feel painful things.

Self-reflection:

Think about how you handle your own triggers or hard feelings. How can you tell your partner about this, and how do you want them to help you?

Practical Guidance:

Approach this conversation with care and make sure your partner feels safe enough to talk about how they deal with stress.

Help them in ways that fit with how they deal with stress.

Holistic Viewpoints:

It's important to respect each other's different ways of coping and be ready to help or give space as needed.

For Long-Term Relationships:

As people grow and change, their ways of dealing with problems may change. Checking in on how everyone is doing can help keep the support system strong and flexible.

Expert Insight:

Everyone has different ways to deal with stress, which may come from their own experiences, their personalities, or advice from a professional. Some people might do better with professional help, like therapy, while others might prefer to think about things on their own or do things they enjoy. The important thing is to accept these differences without judging them and to help your partner in ways that meet their needs.

This conversation is a key part of building a healthy relationship in which both people feel understood and cared for. It might require talking to each other often and being willing to change as both people grow and change. Having this conversation shows that you want to understand and support each other's emotional health, which is a key part of a strong, caring relationship.

CHAPTER NINE

CONFLICT RESOLUTION

HEALING AND GROWTH THROUGH UNDERSTANDING AND FORGIVENESS

Question #47:

How do you handle disagreements or arguments?

Purpose:

With this question, you want to find out how your partner handles disagreements. Their actions can affect how well your relationship works and how long it lasts.

Why It's Important:

This provides insight into a person's conflict resolution skills and emotional maturity, essential for maintaining a healthy relationship.

Possible Answers:

- "I would rather take a step back and calm down before we talk about it."

- "I think disagreements should be talked about directly and solved right away."

- "I try to stay out of fights, so I might need some time to think."

Follow-up Questions:

- Can you share an example of how you handled a disagreement in the past?

- How do you feel after an argument? How do you feel when you have had a fight?

- What do you think makes a disagreement 'resolved'? What do you think makes a disagreement "solved"?

On a Lighter Note:

If they say that when they disagree, they start a dance-off, get ready for some killer dance moves when you argue with them.

Positive and Negative Aspects:

Positive: Emotional intelligence can be seen in how well someone can solve problems in a positive way.

Negative: Avoiding or being mean to someone can lead to unresolved problems or anger.

Self-Reflection:

How do you handle disagreements? Are you happy with the way your partner acts? How could you work together to find good ways to solve problems?

Practical Guidance:

Think about how you handle disagreements on your own. Do you tend to avoid the problem or face it head-on? Are there certain things or patterns that could make a fight worse? Understanding how you react can help you handle conflicts in a more positive way.

Next, talk about how you and your partner have solved problems in the past. What went well and what didn't? Find out what values, fears, or needs are really driving your actions.

During a fight, talk about what you need from each other. This could include specific ways to talk, emotional support, or a place to take a break. Make sure you both feel like you are being heard and treated with respect.

Think about making some ground rules for how to handle disagreements. This could mean not pointing fingers, talking about feelings and needs instead of positions, or agreeing to take a break if things get too heated.

It's also important to realize that disagreements don't always mean that a relationship is bad. Often, they are a chance to learn more about each other and grow as a group.

Holistic Viewpoints:

People have different ways of dealing with conflict based on who they are, what they have done in the past, and where they come from culturally. Some people might like to deal with problems right away, while others might need time to think about it before talking about it. There are also cultural differences to think about. For example, in some cultures, open confrontation is seen as healthy and necessary, while in others, it is seen as rude and is usually avoided. When you ask this question, keep an open mind and try to understand these differences. It is also important to remember that a person's way of dealing with disagreement is not a fixed trait, but something that can change and get better with effort and good communication. Talking about this can help you understand each other better and set the stage for healthy ways to deal with disagreements in your relationship.

For Long-term Relationships:

Even long-term couples face disagreements. Open, honest communication is key. Remember, it's okay to seek help from a relationship counselor if you're struggling to resolve conflicts effectively.

Attachment Styles:

Mary Ainsworth, a developmental psychologist, came up with the idea of attachment styles[1]. These are patterns of how we think, feel, and act in close relationships. They are formed when we are young and affect the way we get along with other people for the rest of our lives.

Secure Attachment Style: People who have a secure attachment style usually try to solve problems in a fair and constructive way. They are more likely to stay calm, listen to their partner's point of view, and talk clearly about how they feel. They may say that they want to find a compromise or a solution that works for both sides. They respect each other and are usually able to talk about problems without pointing fingers or avoiding the issue.

Anxious Attachment Style: People with this style may be very sensitive to arguments and worry that fights will hurt their relationship. They might react to disagreements with a lot of emotion and have trouble calming down quickly. During and after fights, they may want to know that they are still loved and cared for. They might also try to please or appease their partner to get things back to normal quickly.

Avoidant Attachment Style: People with this style might try to avoid conflict at all costs because they see it as dangerous or pointless. When disagreements come up, they might ignore or downplay them, or they might just walk away. They may also prefer to solve problems on their own rather than as a group, which shows that they need space to calm down and think about what's going on.

Disorganized Attachment Style: People with a disorganized attachment style may act in different ways during fights, going back and forth between wanting to be close to their partner and pushing them away. They might have trouble controlling their feelings and

---

1. https://thewaveclinic.com/blog/what-are-the-different-types-of-attachment/#:~:te
xt=From%20the%20observational%20study%2C%20Ainsworth,%2Fresistant%20(
type%20C).

talking to people in a clear way. Their reactions could be anything from strong emotional reactions to completely shutting down.

Expert Insight:

Psychologists suggest using 'I' statements, active listening, and empathy during disagreements. They also recommend resolving conflicts sooner rather than later to avoid pent-up resentment. Remember, the goal is mutual understanding and respect, not 'winning' the argument.

Question #48:

Do you believe in compromising?

Purpose:

This question is meant to find out how willing your partner is to compromise and find a middle ground when you disagree. It is a way to see how well they understand what it means for a relationship to be fair and respectful to both people.

Why It's Important:

Willingness to compromise indicates flexibility and dedication to maintaining harmony, crucial in any partnership.

Possible Answers:

- "Yes, I think it is important for any relationship to be able to compromise."

- "It depends on what is happening. There are certain things I might not compromise on."

- "Compromise is hard for me, but I am willing to learn and get better."

Follow-up Questions:

- Can you share an example of a compromise you've made in the past? Can you give an example of a time when you had to give something up?

- How do you decide when to compromise and when to stand your ground? How do you know when to give in and when to stick to your principles?

- How do you feel when you make compromises? How do you feel when you make a compromise?

On a Lighter Note:

If they believe in compromise so much that they are willing to give you their last piece of pizza, you have found a real keeper.

Positive and Negative Aspects:

Positive: Being willing to compromise shows that you are emotionally mature and want to make decisions that are fair.

Negative: Giving in too much could make you feel angry or like you have lost your identity.

Self-Reflection:

Think about how you feel about making concessions. How do you feel when you make concessions? Are you happy with how your partner handles compromise?

Practical Guidance:

Before you answer this question, you and your partner should think about what compromise means to each of you. It could mean giving up something you want for the sake of the relationship, finding a solution that meets the most important needs of both people or coming up with a creative way to make both people happy.

Think about how you have dealt with compromise in the past. What has seemed fair or good? What hasn't happened? Are there places where it's harder for you to give in? If so, why might that be?

Talk about your expectations for compromise in different parts of your relationship, like making decisions, taking care of responsibilities, having fun, and making plans for the future. How will you handle situations where your wants and needs are at odds?

Talk about what you can do to make sure that compromises are fair and good for both sides. This could mean asking each other for advice, being honest about how you feel and what you need, and being willing to change your minds if a decision isn't working.

Keep in mind that compromising isn't about keeping score or giving in to avoid a fight. It's about working together to make a relationship that fits both of your values, needs, and wants.

Holistic Viewpoints:

The idea that you should compromise is about much more than just giving and taking. It's a way of thinking and a dance that brings together differences in culture, differences in people, and the shadows of past relationships. Not everyone is willing to compromise, and it's not always the same. It can change over time and between different relationships. It takes understanding and empathy to know what compromise means to a partner. It's about understanding the beliefs, fears, and hopes that make people willing or unwilling to meet halfway. At the same time, it requires both sides to be willing to put themselves in the other person's shoes, respecting their comfort levels while finding solutions that aren't just good enough but really make them happy. The idea of compromise is more than just a way to get things done. It touches us deeply on an emotional, psychological, and cultural level.

For Long-term Relationships:

People often say that compromise is the key to long-term relationships and the glue that holds two different people together into a harmonious whole. But, like all deep ideas, it's much harder to do in real life. In a long-term relationship, compromise isn't just a nice thing to do once in a while; it's a constant part of how people live together. It's the small decisions, changes that don't need to be said out loud, and quiet acknowledgments that lead to respect and understanding. But there are risks when you make a deal. There is a fine line to walk between making a healthy compromise and putting yourself down. It's important to be aware of this balance, to realize that one partner might be willing to give up more than the other, and to work on finding balance on purpose. In a long-term relationship, compromise is not a goal but a process that requires constant thought, communication, and, most importantly, a shared belief in the value of being together.

Attachment Style:

Compromise is an important part of any relationship, but a person's attachment style can affect how willing and able they are to compromise. Let's look at how people with different types of attachment deal with compromise:

Secure Attachment Style: People who have a secure attachment style usually do not mind making concessions. They like to talk to each other in an open and honest way and know that healthy relationships need balance and compromise from both sides. These people usually have a high level of emotional intelligence and put the well-being of the relationship ahead of their own goals or winning an argument.

Anxious Attachment Style: People with this style may find it hard to understand the idea of compromise. Their fear of being left alone or rejected might make them give in more than they need to in order to keep the peace, which can make them angry over time. They may also be afraid that if they give in, they will lose the love or attention of their partner. The fact that they are so focused on getting love and reassurance could make negotiations more emotional.

Avoidant Attachment Style: People who have this style can find it hard to make compromises. Because they put a lot of value on being independent and able to take care of themselves, they might not want to make concessions that they see as giving up their freedom. They might avoid or shut down during talks that require compromise. Compromising could be seen as an attack on their privacy and freedom.

Disorganized Attachment Style: People with a disorganized attachment style may not always know how to compromise in the same way. At times, they may seem willing to compromise because they want to be close, but at other times, they may fight it because they are afraid of being close. Their actions in risky situations might be random and based on their different needs for closeness and space.

It's important to remember that these are general tendencies that might not apply to everyone with a certain attachment style. Also, people can change their attachment styles with time and work, especially in a relationship where they feel safe and supported. In a healthy relationship, both people should try to talk about their needs and limits in an open, kind, and respectful way. This makes people feel safe, which makes it easier to find fair solutions.

Question #49:

How would you handle it if we had a conflict that we couldn't resolve on our own? Would you be open to therapy or counseling?

Purpose:

This question finds out if your partner is willing to get help from outside the relationship when things are not going well. It can help you understand how they feel about mental health and how much they want to solve problems.

Why It's Important:

This question reveals one's openness to external help, illustrating their commitment to relationship health.

Possible Answers:

- "I would not mind going to therapy if it could help us."

- "I think we can work out our problems on our own."

- "I do not feel good about therapy, but I am open to looking at other options."

Follow-up Questions:

- Have you ever sought therapy or counseling before? Have you ever gone to a therapist or counselor? If so, how was your experience?

- What are your thoughts on self-help books, workshops, or relationship courses? What do you think about books, workshops, and courses on relationships?

- What are your concerns or fears about therapy, if any?

On a Lighter Note:

Be prepared to embrace the spirit of adventure if they say they are open to couples therapy with a twist, such as skydiving or deep-sea diving.

Positive and Negative Aspects:

Positive: A willingness to invest in therapy and take the initiative to fix issues in the relationship is indicative of these qualities.

Negative: A person's reluctance to engage in therapy could be the result of prejudice, negative experiences, or simply a lack of knowledge.

Self-Reflection:

How do you feel about seeking external help for relationship conflicts? Are you comfortable with your partner's perspective?

Practical Guidance:

Start by talking about how you feel about conflicts that don't seem to go anywhere or can't be solved. What could cause this to happen? What worries or fears does it make you think about?

Talk about how you've handled similar situations in the past, whether they were with this person or with other people. What went right and what went wrong? What might you want to change about how you do things in the future?

Think about how you feel about therapy or counseling. What do you think are the pros and cons? Do people have any wrong ideas or fears about therapy that need to be cleared up?

Talk about how you would choose a counselor or therapist. What skills or qualifications do you think are important? How would you make sure that your needs and values are met during therapy?

Think about how you can make a safe and helpful environment for people who want to get professional help. This could mean talking openly about what you hope to get out of therapy, being patient with each other as you learn a new process, and being involved in the work both inside and outside of the therapy room.

This question is really about how much you care about the relationship and how far you're willing to go to make it work.

Holistic Viewpoints:

Cultural beliefs and societal norms can shape people's perspectives on therapy. Seeking therapy, for example, may be frowned upon or equated with "airing one's dirty laundry" in some societies. In some cases, therapy may be considered only as a last resort. Moreover, the social stigmas and pressures associated with therapy may play out differently for people of different genders. Try to empathize and look into options that are respectful of other cultures if you need to.

For Long-term Relationships:

In long-term relationships, problems can sometimes get so bad that they seem impossible to solve. Communication, empathy, and compromise are all important ways to solve problems, but sometimes a different approach is needed. In these situations, being open to the benefits of therapy or counseling isn't just a way to find solutions; it's also a sign of commitment to the health and longevity of the relationship. This openness should be looked at again and again, because people's ideas about therapy can change over time, with experience, and based on the nature of the conflict. Maintaining a willingness to get professional help if needed shows a commitment to growth, mutual understanding, and the pursuit of a fulfilling relationship built on more than just common interests, but also on shared strategies for navigating the complexities of love and life together.

Attachment Styles:

Secure Attachment Style: When it comes to solving problems in a relationship, people with a secure attachment style are usually open and flexible. They know that asking for help is not a sign of weakness but a way to make the relationship better and stronger. They might be willing to try therapy or counseling if they thought it would help them solve their problems and grow.

Anxious Attachment Style: People with this style may have mixed feelings about counseling or therapy. On the one hand, they could see it as a chance to fix their relationship and make things better, which might make them want to get help. On the other hand, they might worry that asking for help from someone outside the relationship could reveal weaknesses and make the relationship less stable. Their answer might depend on how their partner reacts and what they think the risks and benefits of therapy are.

Avoidant Attachment Style: People with an avoidant attachment style generally value their independence and may be more resistant to the idea of therapy or counseling. They might see it as a violation of their privacy and worry that it will make them lose their freedom. But if they knew that this approach could help them get along better, they might change their minds.

Disorganized Attachment Style: People who have a disorganized attachment style may react more randomly. Depending on how they have dealt with trust and support in the past, they might be open to getting help or they might be suspicious and afraid of it. Their response might depend a lot on how their relationship is going right now and how they are feeling at the time.

Expert Insight:

Many therapists and relationship experts say that suggesting therapy or counseling as a way to deal with unresolved conflicts is not a sign of failure, but rather a proactive and helpful step. Couples counseling is a neutral place where a trained professional doesn't take sides but helps the couple figure out what's really going on and how to fix it. This process can lead to new ideas, teach important skills for resolving conflicts, and even strengthen emotional bonds by helping people understand and care about each other more. Relationship experts often see therapy not just as a last resort, but also as a chance to grow, learn, and make the relationship stronger so it can handle future problems.

Counseling can be a powerful way for both people in a relationship to show how much they value it and how willing they are to invest in its success and happiness.

Question #50:

How do you handle disagreements with friends?

Purpose:

This question helps you figure out how your partner handles conflicts, especially outside of your relationship. It can give you an idea of how well they can handle difficult social situations.

Why It's Important:

It provides a glimpse into a person's social conflict resolution skills, which may reflect their approach to relationship conflicts.

Possible Answers:

- "I tend to avoid conflict, but if something bothers me a lot, I'll speak up."

- "I think open communication is important. If there is a problem, I will try to talk about it and figure out how to fix it."

Follow-up Questions:

- Can you share an example of a recent disagreement with a friend and how you handled it?

- Have disagreements ever led to the end of a friendship for you?

- How do you handle it if a friend is upset with you?

On a Lighter Note:

If they start by saying, "I handle disagreements the same way any mature adult does: I challenge them to a lightsaber duel...", be prepared for a Star Wars marathon in your future.

Positive and Negative Aspects:

Positive: Having a good way to deal with disagreements can help keep and grow friendships.

Negative: Avoiding them could leave problems unsolved and put a strain on relationships.

Self-Reflection:

Reflect on your own ways of handling disagreements with friends. Are there any similarities or differences between your style and that of your partner?

Practical Guidance:

Talk about how you usually settle differences with friends. Do you usually face problems head-on, try to avoid them, find a middle ground, or use some other method? What have you learned from past fights, and how have those lessons changed the way you handle things?

Think about how the ways you handle disagreements with your friends might work in your relationship. How do you plan to help each other and learn from each other as you work through conflicts with friends and with each other?

Think about any worries or fears you might have about having a fight with a friend, especially if it could hurt your relationship. How will you talk to each other and decide what to do about these problems?

Holistic Viewpoints:

How people deal with conflict can be affected by their culture, their personal experiences, or their personality. For example, some cultures may stress open and direct communication, while others may prefer to disagree in a more subtle way. Whether a person's past experiences with conflict were good or bad can affect how they handle disagreements with friends. A person's personality, like whether they are more confrontational or avoidant, can also affect the strategies they use. Respect for these different ways of doing things, along with active listening and empathy, can help people find good solutions.

For Long-term Relationships:

When two people are in a long-term relationship, how they handle disagreements with their friends can tell a lot about how they handle conflicts in general. It's not unusual for these plans to change over time. This could be because of growth, maturity, or changes in values and priorities. So, it can be helpful to talk about how you both deal with arguments with friends and what you can learn from each other. This ongoing conversation helps the two people understand each other better and work together better, which makes it easier to solve problems when they arise within the partnership.

Question #51:

What is a deal-breaker for you in a relationship?

Purpose:

This question is meant to help you find out what your partner thinks is unacceptable in a relationship in terms of behavior, values, or situations.

Why it's Important:

Finding and talking about deal-breakers can help both people in a relationship know what they can and can not do. It can also show problems that might need to be fixed or compromises that should be made.

Possible Answers:

- "Dishonesty and infidelity are deal-breakers for me."

- "Lack of respect and constant negativity are things I can't tolerate in a relationship."

Follow-Up Questions:

- Can you share an example of a deal-breaker from a past relationship?

- Have your deal-breakers changed over time?

On a Lighter Note:

"You have a restraining order against all forms of broccoli? Phew, that's a relief! I thought it was going to be something serious."

Positive and Negative Aspects:

Positive: Knowing the deal-breakers of your partner can help you understand their limits and respect them. This can make your relationship better and more peaceful.

Negative: Something that is a deal-breaker for one partner might be important to the other person's identity or way of life. This could cause problems or even cause the relationship to end.

Self-Reflection:

Reflect on your own deal-breakers. What are the things you can not stand in a relationship? Have you told your partner about these things?

Practical Guidance:

Every person has their own deal-breakers that tell them exactly what they can't stand in a relationship.

Explore each other's deal-breakers and try to figure out the values and experiences that make them what they are. This conversation builds mutual respect and can stop trust from being broken by accident.

Exercise: Write your deal-breakers on different pieces of paper and trade them with someone else. Talk about what you can do to make sure that these limits are respected. Keep talking about this to make sure that these important lines are never crossed.

Holistic Viewpoints:

Deal-breakers can vary significantly based on individual experiences, cultural backgrounds, and personal beliefs. It's crucial to foster a non-judgmental space when discussing these matters and to remember that everyone has the right to determine their own boundaries.

Personal Values: What makes something a deal-breaker often depends on deeply held beliefs, values, and experiences from the past. It can be anything from being dishonest or violent to making choices about how to live or having bad habits.

Cultural sensitivity: Some values or behaviors may be more important in some cultures than in others. It is very important to understand and respect these differences.

Respect each other's deal-breakers. Knowing and respecting each other's deal-breakers builds trust and understanding in a relationship.

For Long-term Relationships:

Over time, deal-breakers can shift and evolve as individuals grow and their circumstances change. Periodically revisiting this conversation can help ensure you're both still on the same page and addressing any new deal-breakers that may have surfaced.

Perspectives Can Change: As a relationship grows, each person's views and needs can shift. What used to be a deal-breaker might not be anymore, and new ones might come up.

Open Communication: Talking about what's important and what shouldn't be crossed on a regular basis can help avoid misunderstandings.

Expert Insight – Attachment Styles:

Conflict Resolution: Recognizing and respecting deal-breakers is important for conflict resolution because it helps people understand their values and needs.

Getting to Know Boundaries: When two people know and respect each other's deal-breakers, their relationship tends to be more trusting and healthy.

Types of attachments:

Secure Attachment Style: People with secure attachment styles may be better able to understand and meet the needs of others. This can help them negotiate and avoid potential deal-breakers.

Anxious Attachment Style: People with anxious attachment may find that a lack of emotional closeness or reassurance is a deal-breaker. They might think that being ignored or not being loved is a very bad thing.

Avoidant Attachment Style: On the other hand, people with avoidant attachment may feel suffocated or annoyed by too much closeness or emotional need.

Question #52:

How do you feel about arguing in a relationship?

Purpose:

With this question, you want to find out how your partner feels about fighting in a relationship.

Why it's Important:

Arguing is inevitable in any relationship. But how disagreements are handled can have a big impact on how well a relationship works and how long it lasts. Because of this, it is very important to know how your partner sees and deals with conflict.

Possible Answers:

- "Arguments are inevitable, but it's important to fight fair and communicate effectively."

- "I prefer to discuss issues calmly before they escalate into arguments."

Follow-Up Questions:

- What strategies do you use to de-escalate arguments?

- How do you approach resolution after an argument?

On a Lighter Note:

"Let's just agree that pineapple does NOT belong on pizza, and we'll never have an argument again!"

Positive and Negative Aspects:

Positive: When handled in a healthy way, arguments can lead to growth, a better understanding of each other, and deeper emotional connections.

Negative: If fighting leads to a lot of negative talk, hurtful actions, or an inability to find a solution, it can hurt the relationship in a big way.

Self-Reflection:

Think about how you usually settle disagreements. Do you try to avoid arguments, or do you think that if they are handled well, they can lead to good things?

Practical Guidance:

Depending on how they are handled, arguments can be good for you or bad for you.

Talk about how you feel about arguments, what you think makes a good argument, and how you like to settle differences. Stress how important empathy, listening actively, and respect are.

Exercise: Act out a disagreement and try to figure out how to solve it. Think about what went well and what could be done better to make sure that your next argument is constructive.

Holistic Viewpoints:

Arguments are a form of human communication that can look very different depending on culture, person, and relationship.

Different cultures may see open disagreement as a sign of honesty and passion, while other cultures may see it as rude. These differences in culture could change how people argue.

Individual Preferences: Your upbringing, past relationships, and personal values all play a big part. For example, someone with an anxious attachment style might see arguing as dangerous, while someone with a secure attachment style might see it as a healthy way to clear up misunderstandings.

Respect: No matter how different people are or how different their cultures are, respect and understanding must be the foundation of any disagreement.

For Long-term Relationships:

Long-term relationships and the way people fight often change over time.

Changes in the relationship: As a relationship develops, the way people fight may change. Unresolved problems could lead to a pattern of avoiding or being anxious. A secure attachment could lead to more open and understanding arguments.

Regular Communication: It can be helpful to take a look at how you fight and what it means for your relationship every so often. When you know and adjust to changes in attachment styles, you can have more productive fights.

Expert Insight:

Dr. John Gottman's years of research give us important information about how couples fight.

Gottman found that successful couples argue in a way that doesn't lead to disrespect or defensiveness. This fits well with the secure attachment style, which focuses on understanding and empathy.

How to avoid the "Four Horsemen"[2] **:** Gottman says that disrespect, criticism, defensiveness, and stonewalling are all bad for relationships. These bad habits can be like the unhealthy ways that people with anxious or avoidant attachment styles might argue.

---

2. https://www.gottman.com/blog/the-four-horsemen-recognizing-criticism-contem
   pt-defensiveness-and-stonewalling/

CHAPTER TEN

BOUNDARIES

DEFINING PERSONAL SPACE AND MUTUAL RESPECT

Question #53:

What are your views on social media usage and boundaries in the relationship?

Purpose:

The goal is to find out how each of you feels about using social media in the relationship and to set clear rules that work for both of you.

Why It's Important:

Social media is a big part of life today. Knowing how each partner sees their role in the relationship can help avoid misunderstandings and encourage a respectful attitude.

Possible Answers:

- "I don't mind if we talk about our relationship on social media, but I'd like to talk about what feels right to post."

- "I'd rather not talk about our relationship on social media and keep it between us."

Follow-up Questions:

- What do you think about tagging each other in posts or photos?

- What kind of content would make you feel bad if it was shared?

- Do you have any rules or expectations for how you talk to friends or followers of the opposite sex on social media?

On a Lighter Note:

If they say, "I only post pictures of my food," they might be a chef hiding in plain sight. Maybe you could do this together as a hobby and start a food blog.

Positive and Negative Aspects:

Positive: Getting everyone on the same page can stop problems from happening.

Negative: If people have different ideas about how to use social media, they might have to work together and keep talking.

Self-Reflection:

Think about your own feelings about social media and how it affects your relationship. What limits are important to you, and how can you tell your partner about them?

Practical Guidance:

Start a conversation about what you both think is and isn't okay to do on social media. Recognize that your points of view might be different and be open to finding a solution that works for both of you.

Holistic Viewpoints:

The way people use social media often shows what they value and what they like in general. Understanding each other's thoughts on this topic can help you figure out how they feel about privacy, sharing, and online manners in general.

For Long-Term Relationships:

Personal views and social media trends can change over time. By talking about this topic often, both partners can keep their social media practices in sync.

Expert Insight on Social Media Etiquette:

In the digital age, it's becoming more and more important to know how social media affects relationships. Some couples use it as a way to show how much they love each other, while others might see it as a chance to fight or not understand each other. Harmony in this area of your relationship can come from clear communication, empathy, and a willingness to negotiate.

A study that was published in the journal Computers in Human Behavior[1] found that using social media decreased the quality of marriages in every model that was looked at. The results of the study show that people who don't use social media are 11 percent happier in their marriages than people who use social media all the time. (Being too busy with social media can make a person forget about their marriage.)

In the end, the most important thing about this conversation is that both sides are willing to understand and respect each other's points of view and find a middle ground that works for both.

---

1. https://www.sciencedirect.com/science/article/abs/pii/S0747563214001563

Question #54:

What personal boundaries are important to you in a relationship?

Purpose:

To understand what your partner needs in a relationship in terms of personal space, privacy, emotional boundaries, and other limits they think are important.

Why it's Important:

Respecting boundaries is essential in any relationship. Knowing what your partner thinks of as their personal limits makes it easier for both of you to respect and understand each other.

Possible Answers:

- "I need some alone time regularly, and it's important for me to maintain individual friendships outside our relationship."

- "I believe in maintaining open communication about our feelings, but I also respect the need for personal space."

Follow-Up Questions:

- Can you give examples of when your boundaries were respected or violated in past relationships?

- How would you communicate your boundaries to me?

On a Lighter Note:

"Remember, when discussing boundaries, it's not like playing a game of 'Operation' where an alarm goes off when you cross one. Unfortunately, life doesn't come with sound effects, so communicate!"

Positive and Negative Aspects:

Positive: Talking openly about limits can help make a relationship healthy and balanced.

Negative: If boundaries are not made clear or respected, it can lead to resentment and tension in the relationship..

Self-Reflection:

Think about your own limits. Are they compatible with those of your partner? Can you respect and understand their boundaries?

Practical Guidance:

Talk about what you've learned, what you value, what you need, or how you feel about personal boundaries in relationships. Focusing on respect, trust, communication, or autonomy can help you figure out what shapes, supports, or tests your boundaries.

Think about how you will handle, honor, or talk about personal boundaries in your relationship. Think about ways to create a space that encourages authenticity, respect, trust, and communication from everyone. What might be involved in terms of mutual understanding, empathy, communication, or setting limits?

Holistic Viewpoints:

People's limits are likely to be very different from one another. People's ideas about what is and isn't okay in a relationship depend a lot on their cultural background, their past experiences, their personalities, and their own morals. To approach the topic with empathy and an open mind, it's important to be aware of how different people are. To understand your partner's limits and communicate your own, you have to work hard.

For Long-term Relationships:

It's important to know that boundaries can change in a long-term relationship. As people grow and change, their needs and level of comfort can also change. Checking in with each other often can help make sure that both people are still happy with the limits that have been set. This practice helps people talk to each other and keeps them from being misunderstood, angry, or accidentally crossing boundaries.

Expert Insight:

People who are co-dependent often find it hard to set and keep healthy boundaries in relationships. Codependency is when a person is too emotionally or mentally dependent on a partner, usually one who needs help because of an illness or addiction. In co-dependent relationships, personal boundaries can get blurry, which can lead to a loss of individuality and a merging of identities that is not healthy. The co-dependent person may give up their own needs, wants, and values to make others happy, which can lead to anger and a loss of self. They might have trouble saying "no" or making their own needs clear. It's important to recognize and understand this pattern if you want to have a balanced relationship where both people can do well. When you stress the importance of clear, respectful boundaries and know how to spot the signs of codependency, your relationship can become healthier and more independent. If you or your partner have this pattern, it may be helpful to get professional help, like therapy with a mental health professional who specializes in co-dependency.

Signs you might be co-dependent:

Excessive Need for Approval: You are always looking for validation and approval from other people, even if it hurts your own health or values.

Struggle with boundaries: You might find it hard to set and keep personal boundaries, and you might often give up your own needs for the sake of others.

Focus too much on other people: Your thoughts and actions are mostly about other people, and you often forget about your own needs, wants, and growth.

Fear of Abandonment: You might be afraid of being rejected or left alone, which could make you go to great lengths to please others or avoid conflict, even if it's bad for you.

Need to Control: You might feel like you have to control other people because you want to avoid uncertainty or bad feelings.

Loss of Identity: You may lose yourself in relationships, putting the needs and wants of others ahead of your own to the point where you can't figure out what you really want or need.

Relationship Problems: Codependency can cause problems in relationships that last for a long time, like not being able to talk openly, having trust issues, or always being tense.

Emotional reactivity: Your feelings may be very tied to the people around you, which can make it hard for you to be emotionally independent.

Denial of Co-dependency: Refusing to admit that these patterns exist in your relationship could be a sign of codependency.

Question #55:

How do you feel about personal space in a relationship?

Purpose:

To understand how your partner feels about the need for independence and space in a relationship.

Why it's Important:

Maintaining your own identity and growing as a person is important in a relationship. This space gives both partners a chance to keep up with their lives outside of the relationship, which makes the relationship as a whole healthier.

Possible Answers:

- "Personal space is crucial to me; we all need time for ourselves."

- "While I appreciate some personal space, I also value shared experiences and time spent together."

Follow-Up Questions:

- How do you define "personal space"?

- How can we respect each other's personal space?

On a Lighter Note:

"Remember, asking for personal space doesn't mean your partner is training to be an astronaut. It's just a simple request for a bit of 'me' time. You'll survive, I promise!"

Positive and Negative Aspects:

Positive: Giving people their own space can help build trust and respect in a relationship.

Negative: When people do not understand each other's needs for space, it can feel like they are being ignored or smothered.

Self-Reflection:

Think about your own needs for personal space. Are they compatible with your partner's needs? If not, can you find a balance that respects both of your needs?

Practical Guidance:

Talk about what you want, what you need, what you value, and how you feel about personal space in relationships. Focusing on individuality, trust, autonomy, and balance, you should try to figure out what shapes, supports, or challenges your need for personal space.

Think about how you will deal with, honor, or balance personal space in your relationship. Think about ways to create a space that encourages personal and group growth, self-expression, trust, and respect. What might be involved in terms of mutual understanding, empathy, autonomy, or communication?

Holistic Viewpoints:

People's needs for personal space are often affected by how they were raised, their culture, their personality, and the things they've done in the past. Some people might think of personal space as time alone to think, do hobbies, or just relax without anyone else around. For some people, personal space may have less to do with physical solitude and more to do with emotional independence. Neither way is right or wrong, but it's important to understand these different needs if you want your relationship to be based on respect and compassion.

For Long-term Relationships:

When people are together for a long time, personal space can become a more complicated issue. Couples often get used to each other's habits and needs as time goes on. Still, a person's need for space can change as their life circumstances, stress, and personal interests change. Couples can deal with these changes by checking in with each other often, having honest conversations, and being flexible. This will help them keep a healthy balance that respects both their togetherness and their individuality. To keep this balance, you may need to make changes often and be willing to talk openly.

Expert Insight:

Relationship experts often talk about how important personal space is. Dr. Terri Orbuch, for instance, says that time apart can make people appreciate the time they spend together more[2]. It lets each person keep their own identity, grow as a person, and bring new energy and ideas into the relationship. Finding this balance can improve both the health of each person and the health of the relationship as a whole.

---

2. Orbach, Terri L. - 5 Simple Steps to Take Your Marriage from Good to Great
   Paperback – 2015

Question #56:

How do you feel about sharing passwords or having access to each other's social media accounts?

Purpose:

The main goal of this question is to find out what your partner thinks about privacy, trust, and limits in digital interactions.

Why it's Important:

In the digital age we live in now, our online lives often feel like an extension of who we are as people. Talking about social media etiquette, privacy, and limits can help both people in a relationship understand and trust each other more.

Possible Answers:

- "I value privacy and trust. I don't think it's necessary to share passwords unless there's a practical reason."

- "I don't mind sharing passwords. I believe it can foster trust in a relationship."

Follow-Up Questions:

- Why do you feel that way about sharing this kind of information?

- How would you handle situations where privacy and trust might conflict?

On a Lighter Note:

"So, you're saying that giving you my social media password also gives you the right to like your own pictures from my account? That's a level of inception I wasn't ready for."

Positive and Negative Aspects:

Positive: If both partners agree on a certain level of openness and mutual respect, it can strengthen trust and reduce misunderstandings.

Negative: If people have different ideas about this issue, they may feel like they are being controlled or mistrusted.

Self-Reflection:

Think about how comfortable you are with sharing and privacy online. What are your limits, and why do you think they are important?

Practical Guidance:

Talk about how you feel, what you value, or what you think about accessing each other's social media or sharing passwords. Think about things like trust, privacy, autonomy, and openness that affect how you feel about this issue.

Explore the underlying values, needs, or principles that might make you feel good about sharing this information or make you feel uncomfortable about it. How will you and your partner handle, respect, and help each other with these parts of your relationship?

Exercise: Think about making a "relationship privacy agreement" that spells out what you both feel comfortable sharing and why. This will help you set clear limits and show each other respect.

Holistic Viewpoints:

When it comes to sharing passwords or having access to each other's social media accounts, people have a lot of different feelings, values, and levels of comfort. The way people feel about privacy, their past experiences, cultural norms, and their own personalities may affect how they feel about this issue. Some people might see this as a sign of trust and openness, while others might see it as an invasion of their privacy. The key is to realize that neither point of view is inherently right or wrong. What works best is a shared understanding and mutual respect for each other's feelings and boundaries.

For Long-term Relationships:

When people have been together for a long time, the dynamics may change. Due to shared responsibilities and other life obligations, you may need access to some shared accounts or information. But even though people live close together, they still need their own space and independence. Talking about what to share, why, and when can be important for getting through this tricky area. It's not just about sharing; it's also about the intention, trust, and mutual agreement behind this choice. And these agreements might change over time, depending on how the relationship grows and changes.

Expert Insight:

Researchers have found out what could go wrong when people in relationships share or watch each other too much. Clayton et al.[3] did a study that was published in Cyberpsychology, Behavior, and Social Networking. It found that these behaviors could cause problems in relationships and make people less happy. Trust, control, and respect are often at the heart of these problems. It's important to find the right balance so that sharing doesn't turn into surveillance and trust doesn't turn into control.

---

3. Clayton, R. B., Nagurney, A., & Smith, J. R. (2013). Cheating, Breakup, and Divorce: Is Facebook Use to Blame?. Cyberpsychology, Behavior, and Social Networking, 16(10), 717-720.

Question #57:

Are there any aspects of our lives that you believe should remain private?

Purpose:

This question is meant to find out how the partner feels about privacy in a relationship and what they think of as their own, shared, and private spaces.

Why it's Important:

Understanding each other's need for privacy can help build trust and respect, which can lead to a healthier and more peaceful relationship.

Possible Answers:

- "I believe we should respect each other's personal space and thoughts unless shared voluntarily."

- "While transparency is important, there might be personal aspects like personal conversations with friends or family that should remain private."

Follow-Up Questions:

- Why do you believe these areas should remain private?

- How can we respect each other's privacy while maintaining openness in our relationship?

On a Lighter Note:

"Are there aspects of our lives to remain private? So, unless you are really interested in how I pick my nose...?"

Positive and Negative Aspects:

Positive: Trust and mutual respect can grow when people know and respect each other's need for privacy.

Negative: If partners have very different ideas about what privacy means, it can lead to disagreements and possibly hurt trust.

Self-Reflection:

Think about the limits of your own privacy. Are there parts of your life that you would rather not talk about with anyone, even your partner?

Practical Guidance:

Talk about how you feel, what you value, and what you need when it comes to privacy in your relationship. Focusing on trust, autonomy, respect, or individuality, you should try to figure out what shapes, supports, or challenges your ideas about privacy.

Think about how you'll handle privacy in your relationship, how you'll encourage it, or how you'll respect it. What might be the shared understanding, trust, respect, or boundaries?

Exercise: Have an open conversation in which you and your partner both talk about the parts of your lives you want to keep private and why.

Holistic Viewpoints:

Privacy is a broad idea that can mean many different things to many different people. What one person thinks of as private and personal, another person might think of as something that can be shared. Culture, family life, past relationships, personal beliefs, and a person's personality all affect how they think about privacy. It's a sensitive subject that can affect a couple's sense of safety, trust, and independence. Seeing and respecting these differences isn't just a matter of personal taste; it's a core part of empathy and respect.

For Long-term Relationships:

As relationships get stronger and trust grows, couples often find that some barriers fall away, which makes them more open and willing to share. But this doesn't mean that the idea of privacy is no longer important. In fact, it may become even more important to respect each partner's individuality and autonomy by keeping clear boundaries. Long-term relationships bring new problems, changes in life, and new needs. All of these things can affect how private the relationship is. Both partners will continue to feel understood, respected, and safe if they talk openly and regularly about their needs, without judging or forcing the other person.

Expert Insight:

It's not just what you think about how important privacy is in relationships; research backs it up. Bevan et al.[4] did a study that was published in the Journal of Social and Personal Relationships. They found that people who thought their partners gave them more privacy were happier in their relationships. This study shows how autonomy, privacy, and happiness are all connected in a relationship. It shows that privacy isn't just about keeping things to yourself; it's also about building trust and making connections that respect each person's boundaries.

---

4. Bevan, J. L., Gomez, R., & Sparks, L. (2014). Disclosures about important life events on Facebook: relationships with stress and quality of life. Computers in Human Behavior, 39, 246-253.

CHAPTER ELEVEN

PERSONAL GROWTH

INDIVIDUAL DEVELOPMENT AS A PATH TO A STRONGER RELATIONSHIP

Question #58:

What is your attitude toward continuous learning and self-improvement?

Purpose:

This question helps you figure out how your partner feels about personal growth and improvement. Are they eager to evolve and adapt, or are they more of a "been there, done that, got the t-shirt" kind of person?

Why It's Important:

A commitment to continuous learning and self-improvement indicates a growth mindset, beneficial for personal and relationship development.

Possible Answers:

- "I'm a life-long learner and constantly looking for ways to improve myself. I never stop learning and am always looking for ways to get better."

- "I learn when I need to, but I do not look for ways to improve myself on purpose."

Follow-up Questions:

- Tell me about a time when you tried to learn something new or get better at something.

- Do you have a list of books or classes you would like to take?

On a Lighter Note:

Imagine them saying, "I'm all for self-improvement, as long as it doesn't involve giving up my dessert. That's non-negotiable."

Positive and Negative Aspects:

Positive: If your partner is interested in improving themselves, they are probably open-minded, flexible, and driven.

Negative: If they don't, they may be happy with who they are, but they could become stuck.

Self-Reflection:

Think about how you learn best. Do you like to learn new things, or would you rather stick to what you already know?

Practical Guidance:

Talk about your beliefs and values when it comes to learning new things and improving yourself. Focus on how you feel about personal development, career growth, hobbies, and learning for the rest of your life. Find out how you and your partner both feel about learning and how you can help each other on this journey.

Consider things like formal education, hobbies, career skills, personal habits, and mindfulness practices as ways you both want to grow and get better. How will you work these things into your relationship, find a balance, or do them together? What kind of mutual support, experiences shared, or understanding might be involved?

Holistic Viewpoints:

Continuous learning and improving yourself are very personal journeys that can look very different for each person. Your partner's way of learning and growing might be very different from yours, but that doesn't make it less valid or important.

Some people might want to go to school, go to workshops, read books, or take online classes. Some people might learn best by doing, watching, and thinking about what they do. Self-improvement can also be done for a wide range of reasons, including career advancement, personal fulfillment, mental stimulation, or even just for fun.

It is very important to understand and respect these differences. People can get frustrated and tense when they judge others or try to force their own way of learning on them. Accepting the different ways people learn can make the relationship stronger by bringing in new ideas and experiences.

For Long-term Relationships:

In long-term relationships, helping each other keep learning and get better is an important part of growing up. If you want to help your partner learn, you need to know what their goals are and help them reach them. You can do this by giving them moral support, giving them resources, or even learning with them.

This also means being aware of how learning and growth can change over time. As your careers change, your interests shift, or your life's priorities shift, so will the way you and your partner approach self-improvement. If you keep the lines of communication open and adjust to these changes, you will grow together instead of apart.

Recognizing and celebrating each other's accomplishments, no matter how small, can also create a good environment for growth. It shows both people that they are important and that their personal growth is valued.

Expert Insight:

Research and experts in personal development emphasize the value of continuous learning, not only for cognitive health but also for overall well-being[1] . Engaging in new learning experiences can keep the mind agile, reduce stress, and contribute to a sense of accomplishment and satisfaction.

Furthermore, studies have shown that learning something together as a couple can be an excellent bonding experience. Whether it's a cooking class, a new language, or even a DIY project, shared learning experiences create common goals, cooperation, and fun memories. It's an opportunity to see each other in a new light, appreciate different skills, and create a shared narrative.

However, experts also warn against placing undue pressure on self-improvement, especially if it becomes a source of stress or comparison. Continuous learning should be about personal growth and enjoyment, not competition or meeting external expectations.

In the Context of a Relationship:

The conversation about continuous learning and self-improvement in a relationship is not just about individual growth but also about growing together. It's about understanding what learning means to each partner and finding ways to support, engage, and sometimes even participate in that journey.

Finding that balance between personal development and shared growth requires empathy, communication, and the recognition that learning is an ongoing, evolving process. It's not

---

1. https://news.uci.edu/2010/03/02/uc-irvine-news-release-learning-helps-keep-brain-healthy/

just about the acquisition of knowledge or skills but about personal growth, connection, and the enrichment of life as individuals and as a couple.

Question #59:

Would you be supportive if I wanted to pursue further education?

Purpose:

This question shows how your partner feels about you growing and changing. It also shows how they feel about giving up things and making changes in a relationship, especially when it comes to your goals and dreams.

Why It's Important:

This indicates their willingness to support your personal growth and potential lifestyle changes.

Possible Answers:

- "Absolutely, your growth is important to me."

- "It would depend on the circumstances and how it impacts our lives."

Follow-up Questions:

- How would you feel if the more I wanted to learn, the less time we spent together?

- Would you be willing to make financial changes to help pay for my education?

On a Lighter Note:

Imagine them saying, "Of course, I'd support you. Plus, it'll give me extra time to catch up on my Netflix queue!"

Positive and Negative Aspects:

Positive: If they say yes, it means they want you to grow as a person and are willing to make sacrifices.

Negative: A hesitant answer could mean that the person is worried about how it will affect their time, money, or way of life.

Self-Reflection:

Think about whether or not you would be willing to help your partner go to school. Would you be willing to make the changes that need to be made?

Practical Guidance:

Have a conversation about how you feel about getting more education, your career goals, your personal growth, or your shared life plans. Find out how getting more education fits with or affects your personal goals, shared priorities, or the way your relationships work.

Think about how you would both plan for and pay for your education, taking into account things like money, time, emotional support, and shared sacrifices. How will you negotiate, talk to others, or work together on this? What kind of shared goals, mutual understanding, or empathy might be involved?

Holistic Viewpoints:

Helping a partner who wants to go back to school is a complicated task that may need emotional, financial, or practical support. If both partners know what support looks like in this situation, the process will go more smoothly for both of them.

Emotional support: When a partner goes back to school, it's important to offer encouragement, empathy, and understanding. Whether it's a degree, a job, or a personal development course, giving praise, listening, and understanding when things get hard can make the journey less scary.

Support with money: Depending on the type of education, there may be a lot of costs. Talking openly and honestly about how to handle these money issues will make sure that there aren't any surprises or problems down the road. Getting everyone on the same page about the budget, sacrifices, or investments will help set realistic goals.

Practical Support: Helping out in a practical way could mean anything from doing more housework to making sure there is a quiet place to study. Real, tangible support can be shown by being aware of how much time and effort education takes and adjusting household duties accordingly.

For Long-term Relationships:

Supporting each other's educational goals is not only a sign of love and trust in long-term relationships, but also a way to help each person grow and adapt to their changing identities.

Being there for your partner as they go through their education can bring you closer together. It lets you celebrate their successes with them, understand their problems, and make memories and experiences with them.

Reassessment and Adaptation: As one partner learns more and changes, their interests, career paths, or life priorities may change. Regular conversations about these changes and what they mean for each person and the relationship as a whole can help people adjust to the new situation without misunderstandings or fights.

Expert Insight:

Helping a partner with their education isn't just a nice thing to do; it's also good for the relationship. A study in the Journal of Personality and Social Psychology[2] shows

---

2. https://www.cmu.edu/dietrich/news/news-stories/2017/august/supportive-spous es-brooke-feeny.html#:~:text=Published%20in%20Personality%20and%20Social,b eing%20and%20better%20relationship%20functioning

that having a partner who is supportive leads to more personal growth, happiness, and relationship satisfaction.

In addition, the learning journey itself can give both partners ideas. Seeing a loved one work hard, overcome obstacles, and reach their goals can inspire the other person to find out what they are capable of. This can create a positive cycle of growth and encouragement.

In the context of a relationship, the decision to go back to school is a big one that can have a big impact on both people involved. If you handle it with compassion, honesty, and cooperation, it can be a source of strength and connection instead of a source of conflict.

By being clear about what support means, what sacrifices it might require, and how to deal with those things together, you can build a strong foundation that helps you grow as a person and makes your relationship more satisfying. It's a true partnership, where each person's success is a shared joy and success.

Question #60:

What steps do you take for personal growth?

Purpose:

The purpose of this inquiry is to learn your partner's thoughts on development and progress. Finding out how they go about developing themselves and whether or not they make time for this is crucial.

Why it's Important:

Relationship health is profoundly affected by a person's level of personal development and growth. A partner who encourages and supports each other's development is likely to enrich a partnership.

Possible Answers:

- "I regularly read books, attend workshops, and reflect on my experiences to learn and grow."

- "I set personal goals and review them periodically to ensure I'm progressing."

Follow-Up Questions:

- How do you measure your progress?

- How has personal growth changed you over the years?

On a Lighter Note:

"Well, my personal growth strategy involves eating pizza - every slice consumed is a step towards a rounder, more fulfilled me. But I'm open to alternative interpretations!"

Positive and Negative Aspects:

Positive: a partner who is invested in their own development adds a dynamic of progress and development to the bond.

Negative: It can cause problems if one partner is focused on improving themselves while the other isn't.

Self-Reflection:

Think about your own approach to personal growth. When you look in the mirror, do you like what you see, or do you wish you could change something? It is crucial to appreciate one another's histories and experiences.

Practical Guidance:

Personal growth is often a sign of self-awareness, motivation, hard work, and toughness, and it can make a person's life and relationships much better.

Look at your ideas, values, and experiences in relation to personal growth. Learn what drives, helps, or hinders your personal growth by focusing on your goals, learning, self-care, or mindset.

Talk about how you'll support, balance, or incorporate your own growth into your relationship. Think about ways to create an environment that helps everyone grow, learn, and express themselves. How could there be mutual understanding, encouragement, or growth?

Holistic Viewpoints:

Personal growth is a very personal journey that is often affected by things like upbringing, culture, personality, life experiences, and individual needs and goals. This is how it turns out:

Diverse Paths: There is no one way to grow as a person that works for everyone. Some may put more importance on spiritual growth than on career advancement, while others may put more importance on emotional or physical health.

Respecting Differences: It's important for partners to understand and respect each other's unique growth paths. This means knowing that what works for one person might not work for another and being open to different ways of doing things and different goals.

Shared and Individual Growth: Couples can grow together in areas they are both interested in, but it's also important to encourage and support individual growth.

For Long-term Relationships:

In long-term relationships, the way personal growth works may change as the relationship changes:

Focus That Changes: As people grow and change, their goals and ways to improve themselves may also change. This is normal and healthy, and if both partners are open and flexible, it can be a good thing for them both.

Supporting each other's growth can be a powerful way to deepen trust and connection in a long-term relationship.

Re-evaluation and re-alignment: It can be helpful to re-evaluate and re-align personal growth goals on a regular basis to make sure that both partners are still on the same path and are still helping each other grow.

Question #61:

How do you deal with constructive criticism?

Purpose:

This question is meant to help you figure out how your partner responds to feedback and criticism. Their answer could show how well they are able to change, learn, and grow in their relationship.

Why it's Important:

A big part of a healthy relationship is being able to both give and take constructive criticism. It makes it possible to grow, get better, and solve problems that might come up.

Possible Answers:

- "I welcome constructive criticism as an opportunity for growth."

- "Initially, it can be hard for me to hear criticism, but I understand its value and try to learn from it."

Follow-Up Questions:

- Can you share an example of when you received constructive criticism and how you handled it?

- How do you like to receive feedback?

On a Lighter Note:

"On a scale of one to 'throwing tomatoes', how do you handle constructive criticism?"

Positive and Negative Aspects:

Positive: A partner who can take criticism well is likely to be open-minded, flexible, and committed to making the relationship better.

Negative: A partner who has trouble with criticism may have trouble communicating and be resistant to change or improvement.

Self-Reflection:

Think about how well you can take criticism. Can you take it in stride, learn from it, and make changes for the better, or does it tend to make you upset or angry?

Practical Guidance:

Most of the time, constructive criticism shows care, growth, learning, and understanding. However, it can be hard and complicated in a relationship.

Talk about what you've learned, what you believe, or how you feel about giving or getting constructive criticism. Focusing on intent, approach, trust, or timing, figure out what helps or hurts effective, respectful, and kind criticism for each of you.

Think about how you will handle, deal with, or use constructive criticism in your relationship. Think about ways to create an atmosphere that encourages respectful, well-thought-out, and growth-focused feedback. What might be involved in terms of mutual understanding, empathy, communication, or setting limits?

Holistic Viewpoints:

Dealing with constructive criticism isn't just about the content of the criticism; it also involves personal values, beliefs, experiences, and cultural context:

Emotional Responses: Some people may find it hard to accept criticism, even if it's helpful, because of their own insecurities, bad past experiences, or certain cultural norms. Taking these things into account can help make criticism more effective.

Individualized Approach: Since people react to criticism in different ways, it can be more effective to take into account the person's personality, needs, and situation.

Growth and Improvement: At the end of the day, the point of constructive criticism is to help people grow and get better. Putting it in a positive light and focusing on specific ways to improve it can make it easier to accept.

For Long-term Relationships:

How constructive criticism is handled in long-term relationships can have a big effect on how the relationship works:

Understanding Each Other: If you know how your partner likes to get feedback, you can give it in a way that is respectful and effective.

Regular Communication: Open and honest communication about what works and what doesn't in terms of criticism can help create a trusting environment where both partners feel safe giving and receiving feedback.

Avoiding Resentment: It's important to be careful with constructive criticism so that it doesn't make people angry. This means picking the right time, tone, and words to say what needs to be said.

Expert Insight:

Experts in psychology and how relationships work have interesting things to say[3] :

Link to Success: Being able to take and use constructive criticism is a good predictor of success in many areas of life. It helps people grow, change, and get better over time.

Skill Development: Learning how to give and take constructive criticism is a valuable life skill that can help with relationships, career growth, and personal growth. You can learn this skill through classes, workshops, or coaching from a professional.

---

3. https://www.psychologytoday.com/us/blog/modern-sex/201705/how-couples-can-use-criticism-constructively

Question #62:

Can you share an example of a significant setback or failure in your life, and how you dealt with it?

Purpose:

The point of this question is to find out how strong your partner is and how well they can deal with problems. Their answer can tell you about how they solve problems, how persistent they are, and how they deal with negative emotions.

Why it's Important:

Life is full of challenges and setbacks. It is important for the health and longevity of the relationship to have a partner who can handle these problems well.

Possible Answers:

- "I failed to meet a major deadline at work once. It was a tough experience, but I learned to manage my time better and communicate proactively."

Follow-Up Questions:

- What did you learn from that experience?

- How do you approach failures or setbacks now?

On a Lighter Note:

"So, did you trip over a banana peel, or did you accidentally set the kitchen on fire while attempting to make a grilled cheese sandwich?"

Positive and Negative Aspects:

Positive: A partner who can handle setbacks with grace and determination shows that they are resilient and have good ways to deal with problems.

Negative: If a partner cannot deal with setbacks or tries to avoid them, it may be a sign that they do not have enough resilience or emotional maturity.

Self-Reflection:

Think about how you have dealt with setbacks and failures in the past. How do you typically respond to them? Do you see them as chances to learn and grow, or do they affect your self-esteem and mood in a big way?

Practical Guidance:

When people talk about setbacks or failures, they often learn a lot about character, resilience, learning, and growth.

Explore a big setback or failure that changed your life by focusing on the situation, how you felt, what you learned, how you bounced back, or how you grew. Figure out how this experience has changed your values, behaviors, or goals.

Talk about how you both deal with setbacks, failures, or challenges, as well as what helps or hurts your ability to learn and grow. Think about ways to build a relationship that grows, supports, and learns from shared or individual failures or setbacks. What might be involved in terms of mutual understanding, empathy, resiliency, or support?

Holistic Viewpoints:

Imagine that someone loses their job, which is a common but often terrible setback. This event can have a big effect on a person's sense of self, their finances, and their overall health and happiness.

Cultural sensitivity: In some cultures, losing a job could be seen as a huge personal failure, which could make a person feel ashamed or embarrassed. In others, it might be seen as a bad situation that gives them a chance to grow.

Emotional support: The person's family and friends should be understanding and helpful, knowing that losing a job is a normal part of life and not a reflection of the person's worth or skill.

For Long-term Relationships:

Communication: The person's partner should create a safe space for the person to talk about how they feel without being judged.

Shared Problem-Solving: The couple could work together to come up with a plan for how to handle the financial effects and how to look for a job.

Reinforce Good Ways to Cope: When people know how each other deals with problems, they can help and encourage each other in ways that are best for them.

Expert Insight:

Building resilience[4] : Being resilient isn't just about getting back on your feet; it's also about adapting and growing. A person can deal with loss and turn it into a chance to grow by getting professional help, joining a support group, or focusing on personal growth.

From a long-term view: Recognizing that these kinds of setbacks are part of the ups and downs of life can help you keep things in perspective. It gives you a chance to rethink your career goals, look for new opportunities, and build on your own strengths.

Self-Care: To deal with stress, the person might focus on self-care activities like exercise, meditation, or hobbies.

---

4. https://www.greatmindsunited.com.au/blog/resilience-and-growth

Question #63:

Are you comfortable seeking help from me when you're in need?

Purpose:

This question is meant to find out if your partner is willing to ask for help when they need it, which can show how open they are and how much they trust you.

Why it's Important:

Being willing to ask for help when you need it can make a relationship stronger and help build trust. It can also show how much your partner values what you have to say and sees you as a support system.

Possible Answers:

- "Yes, I believe in seeking and offering help in a relationship."

- "I sometimes find it difficult, but I understand the importance of reaching out for help in a relationship."

Follow-Up Questions:

- How do you typically ask for help?

- Are there certain areas where you find it harder to ask for help?

On a Lighter Note:

"I'm definitely comfortable asking for help. Like that time when I tried to assemble the IKEA furniture and ended up with a bookshelf that looked more like a modern art piece."

Positive and Negative Aspects:

Positive: If your partner is comfortable asking for help, it means they feel safe enough in the relationship to let their guard down.

Negative: If your partner finds it hard to ask for help, they may have problems with vulnerability, trust, or fear of looking weak, which could cause problems in the future.

Self-Reflection:

Think about how you feel when you need help. Do you feel safe asking your partner for help when you need it? This can help you know what to expect and how to talk to your partner.

Practical Guidance:

Encourage your partner to talk about times in the past when they either asked for help or had trouble doing so. This can help them see their habits and where they might be able to improve.

Holistic Viewpoints:

It's important to understand and respect the different things that make people feel comfortable asking for help:

Influences of culture: In some cultures, being independent is highly valued, and asking for help may be seen as a bad thing. It is important to respect and understand these cultural norms.

Societal Norms: Gender roles and societal expectations can make someone less likely to ask for help, especially if they think it shows they are weak.

Personal Factors: A person's upbringing and past experiences may have an effect on how they feel about asking for help. When you talk to someone with empathy, you can help build trust and comfort.

For Long-term Relationships:

In long-term relationships, it's important to talk to each other and understand each other:

Open Communication: Talking often about when and how to ask for help can make a relationship stronger and more helpful.

Adaptation: Needs and preferences can change over time, so it's important to keep talking and making changes.

Expert Insight – Attachment Styles:

Experts give helpful advice on how to ask for help in a relationship:

In spite of what some people think, asking for help is often seen as a sign of strength because it shows self-awareness and the wisdom to ask for help.

Interdependence: In a healthy relationship, both partners can depend on each other without giving up their independence.

Secure Attachment Style: People with secure attachment are comfortable with both being on their own and being close to others. This means they can usually ask for help without feeling nervous.

Anxious Attachment Style: People with this style may ask for help more often to connect with others or feel better.

Avoidant Attachment Style: People with avoidant attachment tend to value their independence, so they may be reluctant to ask for help, even when they need it.

Disorganized Attachment Style: People with this type of attachment have both anxious and avoidant tendencies, and they may have mixed or conflicting feelings about getting help.

CHAPTER TWELVE

HEALTH AND WELLNESS

A SHARED JOURNEY TOWARD PHYSICAL AND MENTAL WELL-BEING

Question #64:

How important is health and fitness to you?

Purpose:

This question gives you an idea of how your partner feels about health and fitness. The more you learn about their worldview, the better prepared you will be for discussing lifestyle habits and potential shared activities.

Why It's Important:

Health and fitness habits can affect lifestyle choices, daily routines, and long-term health. Discussing this can ensure shared values or respect for differences.

Possible Answers:

- "I try to maintain a balanced diet and exercise regularly."

- "I'm not a gym enthusiast, but I believe in staying active and making healthy choices."

Follow-up Questions:

- What kind of physical activities do you enjoy?

- How do you feel about participating in health and fitness activities together?

- How would you handle health challenges if they arise?

On a Lighter Note:

If they say, "I'm more into fitness... fitness whole pizza in my mouth!", brace yourself for a partner who brings the 'fun' in 'funny,' even if it's at the cost of their six-pack abs.

Positive and Negative Aspects:

Positive: An active lifestyle and healthy choices can contribute to well-being and longevity. Well-being and longevity can be improved by being active and making healthy choices.

Negative: However, differences in fitness levels or health focus can sometimes lead to tension.

Self-Reflection:

How important is health and fitness in your life? How would you navigate differences in this area?

Practical Guidance:

Start by talking about what health and fitness mean to each of you and how they show up in your daily lives and choices about how to spend your time. Are there certain activities, routines, or ideas that help you decide what to do? How do they add to your overall happiness and well-being?

Find out if you have the same goals or values or if they are different. How will you help and encourage each other on your journey to health and fitness? Are there possible disagreements or deals that need to be made?

Think about how health and fitness affect other parts of your relationship, such as time management, activities you do together, and lifestyle choices. How will you manage these parts of your lives and fit them together?

Holistic Viewpoints:

Everyone's health and fitness look different because everyone has different skills, resources, and personal tastes. It's not about fitting into a certain mold, but about being healthy. Some people may focus on cardio, while others may pay more attention to yoga, meditation, or what they eat. People's ideas about health and fitness can also be shaped by their culture, their socioeconomic status, and their own values. It's important to approach this topic with empathy, understanding, and an open mind about what being "healthy" or "fit" means to different people.

For Long-term Relationships:

Our bodies and our health needs change over time. This is especially true as we get older or as our lives change. This means that partners' health and fitness routines may change in long-term relationships. To keep up with these changes, we should keep talking about health and fitness. Flexibility and support can help both people adjust to new routines, do things together, or respect each other's health and fitness choices. Communication about health goals, possible worries, or special dietary or fitness needs can lead to mutual support and encourage a shared or complementary approach to wellness.

Question #65:

Do you have any chronic health issues?

Purpose:

This question wants to find out if your partner has any long-term health problems. It can tell you about possible health problems and how they might affect your lives.

Why It's Important:

Knowing about chronic health issues helps prepare for potential future caregiving roles and understanding any related lifestyle adjustments.

Possible Answers:

- "Yes, I have [chronic health condition], but I manage it with [specific treatment or lifestyle choices]."

- "No, I don't have any known chronic health issues."

Follow-up Questions:

- How does this condition affect your daily life?

- What kind of help might you need to deal with this?

- Because of this condition, have you changed anything about the way you live or do you plan to?

On a Lighter Note:

If they respond, "The only chronic condition I have is being chronically fabulous!", well, who can argue with that? You've got a charmer there!

Positive and Negative Aspects:

Positive: Being honest about health problems shows that you trust each other and can help you both plan for the future.

Negative: It could also bring up worries and fears about how it could affect your life together.

Self-Reflection:

Think about how you would react and change if your partner had health problems. Would you be willing to help and make the necessary changes to your life?

Practical Guidance:

Take the time to talk about any long-term health problems, how they affect daily life, how they are managed, and what kind of help might be needed. What worries or fears might people have about these things, and how can you all deal with them?

Look into what your relationship might be like if one of you has a long-term health problem, such as if there are any restrictions, accommodations, or changes to your way of life that might be needed. How will you talk to each other and figure out how to handle these parts of your lives together?

Think about how your shared values, resilience, and empathy might be affected by long-term health problems. How will you build a caring and supportive relationship that takes these parts of your lives into account and honors them?

By talking openly about a potentially difficult and vulnerable part of your lives, this conversation builds trust and understanding. It also sets the stage for a relationship that is strong, caring, and supportive.

Holistic Viewpoints:

People react differently to long-term health problems. To recognize and work with these conditions, you need to have understanding, empathy, and patience. Also, keep in mind that not all health problems or disabilities can be seen. Some people may have health problems that aren't obvious but still affect their daily lives. Some people may have conditions that need constant care or special attention. It's important to approach a partner's long-term health problems with compassion, an open mind, and a willingness to learn and change.

For Long-term Relationships:

Over time, health conditions could change or new ones could come up. It's important to talk openly about health so that we can help each other. Regular communication about treatment, needs, comfort levels, and any changes that need to be made can help the relationship be more understanding and compassionate. Chronic health conditions can also change daily routines, intimacy, or activities that two people do together. Working through these changes together can make the relationship stronger.

Expert Insight:

To deal with a chronic illness in a relationship, both people need to talk, understand, and help each other. Health psychology and relationship counseling experts often say that trust, understanding, and working together are very important when dealing with long-term health problems. A healthy relationship can be helped by making a supportive environment, setting up clear ways to talk, and including each other in decisions about health. It's also important to find a good balance between being a caregiver and a partner, keeping the romantic and personal parts of the relationship while taking care of a long-term health condition. Therapy or support groups might also help people deal with these complicated situations.

Question #66:

Do you believe in maintaining a balanced diet?

Purpose:

This question helps you figure out what your partner thinks about food. It sets the stage for sharing meals, going grocery shopping together, and maybe even making changes to the way you live.

Why It's Important:

Dietary habits can influence shared meals, grocery shopping, and overall health. It's crucial for planning a compatible lifestyle.

Possible Answers:

- "Yes, I try to eat a variety of foods to get all the necessary nutrients."

- "I believe in enjoying food without overthinking it, but I also try to eat healthy most of the time."

Follow-up Questions:

- Are there any specific dietary restrictions or preferences you have?

- How open are you to trying new foods or cuisines?

- How would you feel about planning meals or cooking together?

On a Lighter Note:

If they say, "I maintain a balanced diet – a cookie in each hand!", you might have a future filled with sweet indulgences!

Positive and Negative Aspects:

Positive: Having similar eating habits can make it easier to plan meals.

Negative: Differences do not have to be a problem as long as people respect each other's preferences and beliefs and make room for them.

Self-Reflection:

What do you think about eating a balanced diet? How willing are you to change your eating habits to fit your partner's?

Deeper Discussion:

Talk about your food preferences and figure out how you can plan meals together despite the differences.

Practical Guidance:

Talk about what a balanced diet means to each of you and how it shows up in your daily eating choices, habits, and ideas. What makes you act the way you do? How does it help you reach your goals and improve your well-being as a whole?

Talk about any beliefs and practices that are the same or different in this area. How will you deal with the different ways you eat or find ways to eat the same things? How will you help each other out and respect each other's needs and wants?

Think about how a balanced diet fits into your shared goals for your lifestyle and your relationship. How will you decide what to eat, make it, and eat it together? How will you balance the needs and wants of each person with the values and goals you all share?

Holistic Viewpoints:

Dietary choices can be affected by many things, such as culture, religion, personal beliefs, health conditions, or ethical concerns. Some people are vegetarian or vegan for moral reasons, while others can't eat certain things because of health problems, and others might only eat Kosher or Halal foods. What makes a diet "balanced" can mean very different things to different people. Respecting and understanding these differences is very important, as is realizing that there is no one way to eat that works for everyone.

For Long-term Relationships:

As people get older or as their lives change, their dietary needs or preferences may change. Some people may become sensitive to certain foods, and others may change what they eat for moral or health reasons. Being open and honest about these changes and willing to make changes to shared meals or eating habits can help the relationship be more cooperative and peaceful.

Expert Insight:

Nutritionists and healthcare professionals often talk about how important it is to eat a balanced diet that fits each person's needs and tastes. Different people have different ideas about what a balanced diet is, but it usually means eating a variety of foods from different food groups in the right amounts. In a relationship, knowing each other's food preferences and needs and finding things you have in common can help you eat and do things together. Planning meals together, making allowances for each other's dietary needs, and enjoying the process of making and sharing food can be good for both your health and your relationships.

Question #67:

How do you manage stress?

Purpose:

This question helps you find out how your partner deals with stress. It is important to know what to expect and how to help when things get tough.

Why It's Important:

Stress management strategies affect a person's emotional stability and coping mechanisms. Understanding these helps provide better emotional support.

Possible Answers:

- "I handle stress by engaging in physical activities like running or yoga."

- "I prefer to de-stress with a good book, music, or a relaxing bath."

Follow-up Questions:

- What are some things that commonly stress you out?

- How do you like to be supported when you're stressed?

- Are you open to trying new stress-management techniques?

On a Lighter Note:

If they quip, "I've been stress-eating a lot of kale lately. Don't worry, it's counterbalanced by the stress chocolate!", you've got someone who knows that laughter is the best stress-reliever.

Positive and Negative Aspects:

Positive: Understanding how each other handles stress can help you give the right kind of support.

Negative: It might get people talking about ways to change their lives or deal with conflicts.

Self-Reflection:

Consider your own stress response and coping mechanisms. Are they compatible with your partner's, and how might you manage stress together?

Practical Guidance:

Share your own ways of dealing with stress, such as specific activities, habits, or changes in how you think about things. How have they changed as time has gone on? How do they fit with your overall values and well-being?

Talk about how you plan to help each other deal with stress in your relationship. What will you do to help identify, acknowledge, and deal with stressors as a group? How will you talk to each other and work together to solve these problems?

Think about any shared activities, routines, or ways to talk about stress that you might want to develop as a way to deal with stress together. How will they help you stay strong and connected as a couple as a whole?

Holistic Viewpoints:

Stress is a very complicated and individual thing. People's ideas about stress and how they deal with it can be affected by many things, such as their personality, culture, past experiences, and current life situations. Some people feel better when they work out, while others find comfort in meditation, hobbies, or social connections. It is very important to understand and respect that people have different ways of dealing with stress and not to judge or force one's own methods on others.

For Long-term Relationships:

Life's demands and challenges may change over time, and what used to stress you out may no longer do so. Also, ways of dealing with stress that worked in the past may no longer be useful or relevant. Regular talks about what's making each partner stressed and how they're dealing with it can create an atmosphere of support and understanding. If one partner's way of dealing with stress causes trouble for the other (for example, by pulling away or doing too much of something), talking about it openly and carefully can help you get through this tricky area. Knowing how stressed each other is and being there for each other when they need it can help keep a relationship healthy.

In a long-term relationship, it might also help to do things together that make you feel less stressed. Shared activities, like going for walks, cooking, enjoying a hobby, or just spending quality time together, can not only help relieve stress but also strengthen the bond between partners. It might also be a good idea to know when you need professional help, like counseling or therapy if stress gets too much or keeps coming back.

Expert Insight - Attachment styles:

Secure Attachment Style: People who have a secure attachment style usually have good ways to deal with stress. This could mean getting help from their partner, their friends, or their family, or doing things they enjoy or find relaxing. They are usually honest about how they feel and don't mind talking to their partner about what stresses them out.

Anxious Attachment Style: People with this style may tend to overreact to stressors and may find it hard to handle things on their own. They might rely on their partner a lot for emotional support and ask for reassurance a lot when things are tough. They might also worry and stress out too much, which could cause problems in the relationship because of stress.

Avoidant Attachment Style: People with avoidant attachment styles often deal with stress by pulling away from others, even their partner, or isolating themselves. They might play down how stressed they are and avoid talking about their feelings or worries because they would rather handle things on their own.

Disorganized Attachment Style: People with a disorganized attachment style may react to stress in different ways and in unpredictable ways. For example, they may sometimes turn to their partner for comfort and other times try to push them away. They may have trouble putting their feelings into words or dealing with stress in a consistent way.

Question #68:

What are your thoughts on mental health?

Purpose:

This question gets to the heart of what your partner knows, thinks, and feels about mental health. It can give you an idea of how they might deal with mental health problems if they come up in your relationship.

Why It's Important:

Mental health views can impact how a person handles emotional challenges and supports their partner's mental health needs.

Possible Answers:

- "I think having a healthy mind is just as important as having a healthy body. Everyone should look after their mental health and get help if they need it."

- "I have had mental health problems myself, so I know how important they are and try to keep myself mentally healthy."

Follow-up Questions:

- Have you or a loved one ever dealt with a mental health issue?

- How would you react if I were dealing with a mental health issue?

- What do you think are some good mental health practices?

On a Lighter Note:

If they say, "My therapist says I have an excellent sense of humor!", you've got someone who's open about mental health and has a good laugh about it.

Positive and Negative Aspects:

Positive: A positive view of mental health can mean that people are willing to talk to each other and help each other.

Negative: Stigmatized views could show a lack of understanding or empathy, which could hurt a relationship.

Self-Reflection:

How do you see mental health? Do you feel comfortable talking about your mental health, and could you help a partner who was having trouble?

Practical Guidance:

Share what you think, what you believe, and what you've learned about mental health. How have they changed the way you think, feel, and know yourself in this area? How do they affect your day-to-day life, your relationships, and how you take care of yourself?

Look into how you will support each other's mental health and make it a priority in your relationship. How will you all figure out mental health problems or needs and deal with them? What help or resources could you ask for or offer?

Think about how your mental health affects other parts of your relationship, like communication, vulnerability, empathy, and resilience. How will you build a relationship that is respectful of and good for both of your minds?

This conversation helps you and your partner understand each other's mental health in a deep and caring way. It lays the groundwork for a relationship that is supportive, nurturing, and safe.

Holistic Viewpoints:

Mental health is a complicated and multifaceted part of a person's overall health that affects people of all ages and backgrounds. It doesn't matter how old you are, what race you are, how much money you have, or anything else. The first step toward getting rid of the stigma surrounding mental health disorders is to acknowledge that they exist and are common. When talking about mental health, it's important to be kind, listen without judging, and talk with empathy. It's important to make a safe place where people can talk about their feelings, fears, and worries without worrying about being judged or misunderstood.

For Long-term Relationships:

In a relationship, a person's mental health can change over time, depending on where they are in life and what is going on. It could be changed by things like a new job, planning for a family, personal growth, getting older, or even something unexpected. To deal with these changes, we need to talk about mental health in a consistent, open, and caring way. It's important to not only notice when one partner might be having trouble but also to help each other in preventative and caring ways. Partners should be willing to get professional help if they need it and do things together that are good for their mental health.

Expert Insight:

When it comes to mental health, expert advice and help can be very helpful. Professional groups like the American Psychological Association say that raising awareness, educating people, and helping people understand mental health can make relationships stronger and people more resilient. Professional counseling, therapy, or even just having access to good information and resources can be a part of a complete mental health plan. When it comes to relationships, understanding and caring about mental health can help build trust, strengthen emotional bonds, and make for a more fulfilling and helpful relationship.

CHAPTER THIRTEEN

LIFESTYLE

CRAFTING A SHARED LIFE THROUGH VALUES, HABITS, AND PREFERENCES

Question #69:

How do you envision us traveling together? Would you prefer adventurous trips, relaxing vacations, or a mix of both?

Purpose:

To know how your partner likes to travel and how they think vacations fit into your life together. Do they see themselves climbing mountains, relaxing on the beach, or trying out strange foods in faraway places?

Why It's Important:

Travel preferences can impact how a couple spends leisure time and their experiences together. Discussing this ensures enjoyable shared experiences.

Possible Answers:

- "I live for adventures! Let's backpack around the world!"

- "I see us on a tropical beach, sipping cocktails and enjoying the sun, sea, and sand."

- "I'd like a mix - some adventure, some relaxation. Balance is key."

Follow-up Questions:

- How important is traveling to you?

- How often would you like to travel?

- Are there any must-visit places on your travel bucket list?

On a Lighter Note:

If they say, "I dream of us bungee jumping off every tall structure we find," you might want to invest in a good travel insurance policy and a lot of pairs of clean underwear.

Positive and Negative Aspects:

Positive: Sharing a passion for travel makes for a memorable bonding experience.

Negative: However, a compromise may be necessary if two parties have vastly different tastes.

Self-Reflection:

How do you feel about your partner's travel preferences? How open are you to trying something new, or would you rather they adjust to how you do things?

Practical Guidance:

Talk about what travel experiences you both enjoyed because they fit with your interests, curiosities, or need to relax. How do you imagine your trips together, whether they will be exciting, relaxing, cultural, or a mix of all three?

Find out how your travel preferences match up or don't. How will you talk about, plan, and talk about these things? What kinds of trade-offs, plans, or thrills might be involved?

Think about what traveling means for your relationship as a whole. How will it strengthen your bond, give you more memories to share, or help you learn more about each other and the world? How will travel fit into the lives and values you share?

Holistic Viewpoints:

People's travel preferences can be very different, depending on things like their past, physical ability, previous travel experiences, cultural background, and personal tastes. One person might like the thrill of mountain climbing or jungle trekking, while another might enjoy a quiet beach vacation or learning about other cultures. Finding a solution that works for everyone may require compromise, empathy, and creativity. For example, a couple might plan a trip that includes both adventurous activities and days to relax or learn about a different culture. Talking openly about each person's hopes, fears, limitations, and expectations can help plan trips that meet both people's needs.

For Long-term Relationships:

People change over time, and so can their travel tastes. Changes in a person's life, like starting a family, getting sick, or retiring, can affect what kind of travel they want to do. Even if you are in a stable part of your life, personal growth or new interests can change your desire to travel. Regular talks about how each person's travel interests might be changing can keep travel an exciting and rewarding part of a relationship. For example, if one partner gets interested in cooking, planning trips that include cooking classes or food tours could become a new way to spend time together. Being willing to try out new places or ways to travel together can keep this part of a relationship interesting and fun.

Expert Insight:

Relationship studies, like those in the US Travel Association[1], have shown how important it is for couples to travel together. But traveling itself isn't the only thing that can make a couple happier. It's also how they plan, experience, and talk about their trips. This means taking the time to learn about each other's travel preferences, finding ways to respect those preferences, and being open to trying new things. Even planning for and dreaming about future trips can bring people closer together and make them happier. Some couples may find it helpful to talk to travel guides or experts who know how to make trips that are both exciting and relaxing, or that fit their particular interests or needs.

In the end, the best way to travel as a couple is to talk to each other, show empathy, be flexible, and be willing to explore and grow as individuals and as a pair. Whether you're going on an exciting adventure, a relaxing vacation, or a mix of the two, the journey itself can be just as rewarding as the destination.

---

1. https://www.ustravel.org/sites/default/files/media_root/5.2015_Relationship_Ex ecSummary.pdf

Question #70:

Do you prefer city life or country life?

Purpose:

Find out if your potential life partner prefers the hustle and bustle of the big city or the peace and quiet of the country.

Why It's Important:

Residential preferences can greatly affect a couple's lifestyle and future plans. Understanding this helps align living expectations.

Possible Answers:

- "City life all the way. I enjoy being in the middle of the action.

- "The peaceful country life with open fields and clean air is my ideal."

Follow-up Questions:

- What draws you to your preferred setting?

- Have you ever experienced living in the other setting, and how was it?

On a Lighter Note:

If they say, "I want us to live in the middle of a city so noisy that even the squirrels wear earplugs," perhaps it's time to consider investing in a high-quality pair of noise-canceling headphones!

Positive and Negative Aspects:

Positive: Choosing a new place to live can be less stressful if both parties are on the same page about their ideal living situation.

Negative: However, when people with different opinions have to talk, it often leads to productive compromise discussions.

Self-Reflection:

Is the way you want to live compatible with the way they want to live? Would you rather live in a city with tall buildings or a rural area with rolling hills?

Practical Guidance:

Talk about what it means to you both to live in the city or the country, taking into account your lifestyle choices, values, comforts, or needs. What do you like about living in the city or the country, and why?

Find out how your tastes match or don't match. How will you negotiate, adapt, or fit these ways of living into your lives together? What might be needed in terms of compromises, growth, or understanding?

Think about what your living choices mean for your relationship as a whole. How will they change your relationships, your community, your well-being, or the things you do together? How will you help them grow and change together?

Holistic Viewpoints:

People have many different reasons for wanting to live in the city or in the country. They might be shaped by where someone grew up. For example, people who grew up in rural areas might feel a strong connection to the land, while people who grew up in cities might be drawn to the busyness of city life. Personal values can also be a factor. Some people value the conveniences and cultural opportunities of city life, while others are attracted to the peace and closeness to nature that comes with living in the country. Preferences can also be affected by things that happened in the past, like good memories of a certain place. Communication is the best way to figure out where these preferences come from and find a way to live together that works for both people.

For Long-term Relationships:

People can change their minds about where they want to live over time. People's priorities and wants can change when they start a family, change careers, retire, or even as their own interests and values change. What once seemed like the perfect urban loft might not be so great when you have kids, and a quiet country home might feel lonely when you retire. By talking openly about these changes, you can make sure that both partners feel heard and that any changes to your living situation are made carefully and with cooperation. Sometimes, going to new places together, making connections with people in the community, or finding ways to combine city and country life (like having a city home close to natural areas) can help.

Expert Insight:

Even though the running joke about how people in the country are happier with their lives and people in the city can get better sushi is meant to be funny, it does show that there are real differences between city and country life. Studies like those in the University of British Columbia and McGill University[2] might show that things like community cohesion, access to open spaces, and a slower pace of life make people happier in rural areas. There may be benefits to living in a city, such as cultural diversity, convenience, job opportunities, and, yes, delicious food.

In reality, there isn't a clear choice between living in the city or in the country. Instead, there is a spectrum, with suburban and small-town living offering a mix of city and country features. Working together to figure out what each partner values most about living in the city or the country and finding ways to include those things in shared life can lead to a good compromise. Getting help from professionals like real estate agents who know the ins and outs of different places to live could also be a good way to find the right balance.

---

2. https://www.cbc.ca/news/canada/british-columbia/the-happiest-people-live-in-ru ral-areas-study-finds-1.4671580

Question #71:

How can we accommodate each other's routines and schedules, especially if they are different (e.g. if one of us is a morning person and the other a night owl)?

Purpose:

To figure out how to bring your two separate schedules into harmony. Do you want to spend your life sharing sleepy goodnight kisses and late-night meals?

Why It's Important:

Synchronized routines make daily life smoother and foster mutual respect for each other's time and space.

Possible Answers:

- "I believe that we should honor each other's unique rhythms while also identifying convenient times for us to interact."

- "I believe in the power of adaptability. We could alternate our schedules."

Follow-up Questions:

- What does your daily routine look like now?

- How flexible are you with changing your routine?

On a Lighter Note:

If they say, "I usually start my day when the rooster crows and end it when the sun is high," you may want to make sure there's a good supply of coffee (or earplugs) in your future together!

Positive and Negative Aspects:

Positive: Different daily habits can coexist peacefully if people can learn to communicate with one another.

Negative: However, if the differences are significant, it may be necessary to make some concessions or alterations.

Self-Reflection:

If your partner wanted you to change your habits, would you be okay with that? What elements of your daily schedule are non-negotiable?

Practical Guidance:

Share your own routines or schedules that are based on your lifestyle, work, or personal choices. How do their different sleep and work schedules, for example, work with or against each other?

Find out how you will adjust, negotiate, or work with each other's habits. How will you plan time together, take care of everyone's needs, and find things you all have in common? What kind of creativity, flexibility, or understanding might be needed?

Think about what routines mean for your relationship as a whole. How will they change your relationships, the way you live together, or your own happiness? How will you change, talk to, or help them grow together?

Holistic Viewpoints:

Getting along with different habits and schedules, especially different sleep patterns like waking up early or staying up late, is a difficult and often overlooked part of living with someone else. Biological rhythms often affect how people act at different times of the day, which can be hard to change. Trying to change each other to fit a perfect plan can cause frustration, anger, and other bad feelings.

Understanding that these differences aren't "right" or "wrong," but just different ways that people work can help people be more willing to make accommodations. Recognizing these differences and trying to find ways to coordinate the parts of the day when people do the same things (like meals, social time, etc.) can be more helpful. If one partner likes to get up early and the other likes to stay up late, a good strategy can be to spend time together when they are both awake and respect each other's sleep needs.

For Long-term Relationships:

Changes in work schedules, the birth of children, new responsibilities, and even health issues can all change how people live their daily lives. As these things happen, old ways of getting along with each other might not work anymore. If you talk to each other often and openly, you can adapt to each other's changing needs. This could mean rethinking how chores are done around the house, making changes to family schedules, or even making physical changes to the living space to accommodate different routines (like soundproofing a room for a night owl who likes to watch TV late).

Expert Insight:

Aside from the expected comment about snoring, research[3] does show that couples who sleep in similar ways tend to be happier with their relationships. But correlation doesn't always mean causation, and it's not just having similar schedules that makes people happy. It's how those schedules are managed that makes people happy.

Different schedules don't have to make it hard to be happy in a relationship if they are dealt with with understanding, creativity, and regular communication. Strategies could

---

3. https://www.naturalawakenings.com/2015/07/31/225081/happy-couples-sleep-c loser-together-proximity-at-night-linked-to-contentment-in-relationships

include doing things together like having coffee in the morning or going for a walk in the evening. Couples therapy or coaching could also give advice that fits the needs of a certain couple.

In conclusion, the best way to deal with different routines and schedules is to realize that these differences are often deeply rooted and hard to change. Focusing on understanding, communication, flexibility, and finding shared moments within those differences, instead of trying to get rid of the differences themselves, can lead to more peaceful coexistence.

Question #72:

How important is cleanliness and organization to you?

Purpose:

To see how much of a neat freak your partner is. Which of Marie Kondo and Oscar the Grouch would you rather have as a roommate?

Why It's Important:

Differences in cleanliness and organization habits can lead to daily friction. Discussing this can ensure mutual respect and compromise.

Possible Answers:

- "For me, a clean home is a reflection of a clear head. Organization is key."

- "I am not terribly concerned with cleanliness. Life is too short to stress over a few misplaced socks."

Follow-up Questions:

- What are your housekeeping habits?

- How do you feel about sharing chores?

On a Lighter Note:

If they reply with, "I believe in the five-second rule. Or was it the five-day rule?", you might want to invest in a good mop and some patience (or hazmat suit).

Positive and Negative Aspects:

Positive: Having a common standard for cleanliness can help family members get along.

Negative: The "dirty dishes" argument, however, could arise from having different standards.

Self-Reflection:

What are your cleanliness habits? Are you willing to compromise on your standards of cleanliness if it means making your partner happy?

Practical Guidance:

Talk about what cleanliness and organization mean to each of you, based on your values, comforts, or needs as a couple. How do they show up in your daily life, the places you share, or your own habits?

Find out how your tastes match or don't match. How will you work together to meet each other's needs for cleanliness and organization? What kinds of compromises, agreements, or joint efforts might be needed?

Think about how cleanliness and organization affect your relationship as a whole. How will they change your relationships, the way you live together, or your own happiness? How will you care for, talk to, or help them grow together?

Holistic Viewpoints:

Many things, like a person's upbringing, cultural background, past living experiences, and even personality type, can affect how clean and organized they like things to be. It's important to realize that these preferences are often deeply rooted parts of a person's identity, not just whims. This is why one person's mess could be another person's cozy place to live.

When you look at these differences with understanding and empathy, you try to figure out why people have these preferences instead of just trying to change them. When you talk about what cleanliness and organization mean to you in an open and nonjudgmental way, you can come to a shared understanding and agreement. For example, a minimalist might learn to like some homey touches, and someone who likes a lot of stuff might learn how a clean space helps their partner think more clearly.

For Long-term Relationships:

As time goes on, people's habits, preferences, and even abilities can change when it comes to cleanliness and organization. Maybe a neat-freak phase ends or a person who used to be messy becomes more organized because of their job or their health. Checking in with each other about how they feel about how clean the house is and what might need to be changed can help both partners feel comfortable and respected.

It's important to remember that these changes can be subtle, and making assumptions about what's "normal" or okay for each partner can lead to misunderstandings. This can be avoided by talking about expectations and feelings about cleanliness often.

Expert Insight:

A complex psychological truth is shown by the fact that a person who is too neat might be seen as controlling while a person who is too messy might be seen as not caring. How we take care of our living spaces does show what we value, how much we care, and how much we think of others. The key is to find a middle ground that meets the needs of both sides.

Experts[4] often suggest that couples talk about cleanliness and organization standards and even sign a contract about them. This could mean figuring out who is responsible for what, hiring outside help if needed, or setting aside time to clean together.

But the idea goes further. Finding the right balance between clean and comfortable can be a way to talk and even connect with someone. Working together to make a shared living

---

4. Carlson, D. L., Miller, A. J., & Rudd, S. (2020). Division of housework, communication, and couples' relationship satisfaction. Socius, 6, 1-17.

space that fits both people's needs and tastes can be a great way to get closer and show more respect for each other.

In short, cleanliness and organization are important in a relationship for reasons that go beyond looks or preferences. It talks about individuality, communication, mutual respect, and building a life together. If you approach these issues with empathy, an open mind, and a willingness to negotiate, you can turn a possible fight into a chance to grow and connect.

Question #73:

How will we divide household chores?

Purpose:

To know what your partner thinks about how you should share household duties. This also starts a conversation about how each person likes things to be kept clean and organized.

Why it's Important:

When people share a living space, they have to share responsibilities. It is important to figure out how to divide up the work in a fair and agreeable way since unresolved issues about household chores can often lead to frustration and fights.

Possible Answers:

- "I believe in an equal division of chores, or we can assign chores based on preferences and strengths."

- "We could consider a chore schedule or rotate tasks so that both of us contribute equally."

Follow-Up Questions:

- What are your expectations about my role in household chores?

- What chores do you enjoy, and which ones would you rather avoid?

On a Lighter Note:

"I don't mind vacuuming... as long as it's not my bank account we're talking about!"

Positive and Negative Aspects:

Positive: Talking openly about how chores will be done can lead to a balanced and happy living situation where both people feel valued and happy.

Negative: Different ideas about how to keep things clean and organized and how to divide up chores can lead to fights.

Self-Reflection:

Think about your own habits and preferences. Are you tidy and well-organized, or are you a bit messy? Do you like some chores more than others? Thinking about these things will help you figure out what you like and how to say it.

Practical Guidance:

Sharing household chores is an important part of living together because it affects daily life, the way relationships work, and mutual respect.

Talk about how you would like to share housework, what you expect, or what you value. Learn about your own habits, strengths, and needs when it comes to taking care of housework. Find out where you agree or disagree and how that might affect how you do your chores.

Think about ways you can work together to plan, negotiate, and check in on a fair and satisfying way to divide up household chores that fits your needs and values. Find out what kind of flexibility, cooperation, or shared vision might be needed. Think of ways to make chores something you can do together and enjoy, instead of something that makes you fight.

Holistic Viewpoints:

The way housework is divided should be fair and balanced, taking into account a number of things:

Gender equality means that tasks aren't split up based on stereotypes, but on preferences, skills, and availability.

Communication and Compromise: Partners can find a fair division that takes into account each person's preferences and strengths by talking to each other and being willing to negotiate.

Respect and Understanding: Recognizing and appreciating each other's contributions to running the house helps build mutual respect and teamwork.

For Long-term Relationships:

In long-term relationships, the way housework is divided can change:

Patterns: As a couple lives together for a while, they may find ways to divide chores that work well for them. Still, it's good to look at these patterns every so often to make sure they are fair and everyone is happy.

Adapting to Changes: Big changes in your life, like getting a new job or having kids, may require you to look at how you divide up household chores and make changes.

Shared Responsibility: Talking about teamwork and how everyone has a part to play can help people understand and be happy.

Expert Insight:

Academic research and the insights of professionals provide important context:

Research shows that an unequal division of chores can lead to dissatisfaction and conflict in a relationship[5].

---

5. Does Unequal Housework Lead to Divorce? Evidence from Sweden - Bianchi et al., 2000; Bittman et al., 2003; Brines, 1994; Gupta, 2007; Gupta and Ash, 2008; Lively et al., 2008, 2010

   https://journals.sagepub.com/doi/full/10.1177/0038038516674664#:~:text=Cou ples'%20divisions%20of%20household%20labour,Yogev%20and%20Brett%2C%20 1985).

Importance of Fairness: It may be more important to have a sense of fairness than to have strict equality. Partners may have different ideas of what's "fair," so it's important to be able to talk and understand each other.

Professional Help: Couples who are having trouble in this area might benefit from professional counseling to help them figure out what the real problems are and how to solve them.

Question #74:

Are you a pet person?

Purpose:

Here, you want to find out how your partner feels about animals, especially pets. This can be a big topic of conversation if one of you has a pet or is thinking about getting one.

Why it's Important:

Pets can be fun, give you company, and make you feel like you are both responsible for something. They also take time, money, and work, and not everyone likes them. It is very important to have this talk to avoid future arguments.

Possible Answers:

- "Yes, I love animals and enjoy having pets."

- "No, I don't feel comfortable around animals."

Follow-Up Questions:

- What pets have you had before?

- How do you feel about the responsibilities that come with having a pet?

On a Lighter Note:

"So, are you more of a 'paws and purrs' or a 'slithers and hisses' type of person? Or perhaps you prefer a pet rock—it's low maintenance and very quiet."

Positive and Negative Aspects:

Positive: Sharing a love of pets can bring two people closer together.

Negative: If one partner loves pets a lot and the other is allergic to them or does not like them, it can cause fights.

Self-Reflection:

Ask yourself if you like pets or not. Do you think of your pets as members of your family or just as pets? What kind of pets do you like best?

Practical Guidance:

Talk about what you've learned, what you like, what you value, or how you feel about pets. Figure out what about your lifestyle, responsibilities, connections, or limitations makes you want or not want a pet.

Think about how your relationship and daily life might be different if you like pets or not. Think about how you and your partner agree or disagree about pets and what kind of compromises, understanding, or shared experiences might be needed.

This conversation makes it easier to understand each other's lifestyle choices and emotional needs, which can lead to a more peaceful place to live and a deeper emotional connection.

Holistic Viewpoints:

Keep in mind that some people might not like animals because they have had bad experiences with them in the past or because they have allergies that make it hard for them to live with them. Some may come from places where pets are not usually kept in homes.

For Long-term Relationships:

If you're in a relationship, it's important to talk about how each person feels about pets. It can change where people live, what they do every day, and even where they go on vacation.

If both partners want a pet, it's important to talk about and divide the responsibilities that come with caring for the pet. It helps make sure the pet gets the care it needs and keeps people from getting angry or confused.

Expert Insight:

Pets as Emotional Support: Studies have shown that pets can be a great source of emotional support and friendship[6]. They can make you less stressed, happier, and even better for your body.

But owning a pet also comes with responsibilities and costs, such as food, grooming, veterinary care, and time.

---

6. https://www.popsci.com/environment/emotional-support-animals/#:~:text=The %20study%2C%20which%20was%20conducted,no%20formal%20training%20or% 20certification.

Question #75:

How would you manage potential allergies or health issues related to pets?

Purpose:

To know how your partner would handle health problems that could come up from having pets, such as allergies, diseases that can be spread from animals to humans, or general health concerns.

Why it's Important:

Pet allergies are common and can make it hard for a couple to get together if one person wants a pet. Knowing how you both plan to handle this possible situation can stop you from fighting in the future.

Possible Answers:

- "We could look into hypoallergenic pets or ensure that our home is regularly cleaned to manage allergies."

- "If a severe allergy or health issue arises, we might need to reconsider having a pet."

Follow-Up Questions:

- Have you had to deal with this issue before? If so, how did you manage it?

- How would you feel about rehoming a pet if serious health issues arise?

A Spoonful of Sugar:

"If you're allergic to cats, remember that there are other pets available. You could consider a pet turtle, for instance. They're slower, less fluffy, and they hardly ever climb your curtains!"

Positive and Negative Aspects:

Positive: Having a plan can make sure that both people feel comfortable in their living space and that the pet is well cared for.

Negative: If your partner does not want to or cannot deal with health problems that could be caused by pets, this could cause problems.

Self-Reflection:

Think about your own health and how comfortable you are. Are you willing to make changes if your partner has pet-related allergies or other health problems?

Practical Guidance:

Taking care of allergies or health problems that might be caused by pets is a practical and kind way to live together and stay healthy.

Talk about your experiences, worries, or needs with allergies or health problems that might be caused by pets. Learn what precautions, changes, or things to think about might be needed to deal with allergies or health problems.

Think about ways you and your roommates can work together to design, negotiate, and check in on a fair and satisfying living space that fits both your needs and values about pets and health. Find out what kind of flexibility, cooperation, understanding, or shared responsibility might be needed.

Question #76:

How do you feel about aging?

Purpose:

This question is meant to find out what your partner thinks and feels about getting older, which can be a big part of how well you two will get along in the long run and how you will plan for the future.

Why it's Important:

Aging is a natural part of life, and everyone has their own thoughts and fears about it. If you know how your partner feels about getting older, you can learn about how they feel about life, health, work, and relationships in general.

Possible Answers:

- "Aging is a natural process that I accept. It's more about how you feel than the number of years."

- "I have some anxieties about aging, but I also see it as an opportunity for growth and wisdom."

Follow-Up Questions:

- What are your fears or concerns about getting older?

- What are you looking forward to as you age?

On a Lighter Note:

"Well, they say age is just a number, but I'm also aware that it's a number that keeps increasing every year."

Positive and Negative Aspects:

Positive: If your partner has a healthy outlook on getting older, it means they are likely to take steps to make sure they stay healthy and happy as they age.

Negative: If your partner has a bad attitude about getting older, they may have trouble with their self-image, health, and happiness as they age. This can change how they feel and how your relationship works with them.

Self-Reflection:

Think about what you think about getting older. Are you afraid or open-minded? What do you do to make sure you age well? Your point of view can help set the tone of your talks.

Practical Guidance:

This conversation should be started with understanding and an open mind. Try to get to the bottom of what your partner is worried about when it comes to aging, whether it is health, looks, or something else.

Holistic Viewpoints:

To understand aging, you need a nuanced approach that takes into account personal, cultural, and social factors:

Different cultures may have different ideas about aging. Some cultures may value the wisdom of the elderly, while others may value youth.

Personal Experiences: Aging can make people feel different things depending on their health, career, family life, and how they've been treated because of their age.

Societal Norms: How society views aging and how much the media emphasizes youth can have a big effect on how people feel about getting older.

For Long-term Relationships:

When two people have been together for a long time, they need to talk and help each other:

Conversations That Change: As a couple ages together, they may face new problems, health issues, or opportunities that should be talked about openly.

Emotional Support: Both partners need emotional support as their looks, health, and roles in society change.

Planning for the future: As a couple ages together, it's important to talk about retirement, finances, health care, and other things that will happen in the future.

Expert Insight:

Psychologists and other experts in the field have a lot to say about aging[7]:

Studies have shown that having a positive attitude about aging can lead to better mental health, a better sense of well-being, and even longer life.

Aging Gracefully: Embracing the aging process and finding happiness along the way can make your life richer and more satisfying.

Health Matters: It's important to pay attention to your physical health and make lifestyle choices that support healthy aging.

---

7. https://www.hsph.harvard.edu/news/hsph-in-the-news/positive-attitude-about-aging-could-boost-health/

Question #77:

What kind of lifestyle do you aspire to?

Purpose:

This question is meant to find out what your partner wants out of life in the future, such as where they want to live, what they want to do every day, and what kind of luxuries they want.

Why It's Important:

Lifestyle aspirations influence daily routines, future plans, and overall happiness. Alignment in this area contributes to long-term relationship satisfaction.

Possible Answers:

- "I see myself living in a quiet house in the country where I grow my own food and bake bread."

- "I want to live in a busy city where I can travel a lot and eat at nice restaurants."

Follow-up Questions:

- What factors influenced your desired lifestyle?

- How flexible are you with your envisioned lifestyle, and are you open to compromising?

On a Lighter Note:

If they say, "I want to live like a hermit in the wilderness, with no human contact," you might want to discuss the logistics of visiting civilization for date nights.

Positive and Negative Aspects:

Positive: Having the same ideas about how to live can be a sign of compatibility.

Negative: But if people have very different lifestyle goals, they might need to talk about it and possibly find a middle ground.

Self-Reflection:

How does the life your partner wants to live match up with the life you want? How willing are you to change or adjust the way you live?

Practical Guidance:

Share what choices in your life make sense to you and reflect your values, goals, or well-being. How do you see your daily life, the balance between work and life, involvement in the community, or personal growth?

Find out if your lifestyle goals are similar or different. How will you talk about, support, or work these things into your lives together? What kinds of concessions, changes, or growth might be needed?

Think about how your lifestyle choices affect your relationship as a whole. How will they affect your connection, your happiness, or the things you do together? How will you help them grow and change together?

Holistic Viewpoints:

Aspirations for a good life are not the same for everyone. What's interesting to one person might not be at all interesting to another. Most of the time, the differences come from different cultures, upbringings, personal experiences, and values. For example, one partner might want to live a nomadic life full of travel and adventure, while the other might want stability and a close-knit group of friends. To understand these preferences, you need to talk to each other openly, show empathy, and accept that it's normal to have different goals. Instead of just focusing on what's different, it might be better to look for things you have in common or ways to combine different parts of your lifestyle goals.

For Long-term Relationships:

People's goals for their lives can change a lot over time. Changes in a person's life, like getting a promotion at work, becoming a parent, or even retiring, can change what they value in their daily life. If these changes aren't made clear, they can cause tension. Talking about how and what each person is feeling and wanting on a regular basis can help people understand each other and work together. For example, if one partner's new interest in protecting the environment makes them want to live more sustainably, talking about how to do this can help both partners feel connected to this new goal. To adapt to these changing goals, you need to be flexible and talk to people often.

CHAPTER FOURTEEN

LOVE AND AFFECTION

KEEPING THE SPARK ALIVE IN EVERY STAGE OF RELATIONSHIP

Question #78:

How do you express love?

Purpose:

By asking this, you can learn more about your partner's preferred method of expressing their feelings for you. Having this awareness can help eliminate barriers in communication and open the door to a more profound emotional connection.

Why It's Important:

Understanding each other's love languages helps ensure emotional needs are met, fostering a stronger bond.

As per Dr. Gary Chapman's *The Five Love Languages*[1] , here are brief descriptions and examples of the five primary ways people prefer to receive love:

- **Words of Affirmation:** Verbal acknowledgments of affection, including frequent "I love you's", compliments, and words of appreciation.

- **Acts of Service:** Actions, rather than words, are used to show and receive love. Cooking a meal, doing the laundry, or picking up a prescription are all acts of service.

- **Receiving Gifts:** Gifting is symbolic of love and affection. They don't have to be expensive or elaborate—it's the thought that counts.

- **Quality Time:** This language is all about giving the other person your undivided attention.

- **Physical Touch:** This love language includes any form of physical touch with the intention of showing love and affection.

Possible Answers:

- "I express love through words of affirmation."

- "Acts of service are my way of showing love."

- "I love spending quality time with my partner."

Follow-up Questions:

- Can you share examples of how you've expressed love in previous relationships or in your current relationship?

- How do you like to receive love?

- Are you willing to express love in ways that your partner most appreciates, even

---

1. Chapman, Gary (2004) The Five Love Languages: The Secret to Love That Lasts. ASIN B079B7PJMV

if they're different from your own love language?

On a Lighter Note:

If they say their love language is car maintenance, prepare for some slippery garage floors and greasy clothes!

Positive and Negative Aspects:

Positive: When people know how the other person expresses love, they can feel closer and happier.

Negative: But if mismatched love languages are not talked about openly, they can lead to misunderstandings or feelings of being ignored.

Self-Reflection:

What's your love language? Are you comfortable with the way your partner expresses love?

Practical Guidance:

Talk about the specific things people do, say, or do not do that make you feel loved. Is it through physical touch, words of affirmation, acts of service, getting gifts, or spending quality time together? How have you shown love in the past, and how might you want to show it this time around?

Tell each other about times when you felt loved and valued by the other person. What specifically made you feel that way?

Talk about anything that might make it hard for you to show love the way you want to. Are there worries or fears that need to be dealt with?

Think about making an agreement about how you'll show each other love, respecting each other's tastes, and pushing each other to grow in areas where you might feel less comfortable.

Holistic Viewpoints:

To understand how people show love, you need a deep and multifaceted understanding of the many things that shape this basic human emotion. People's love languages, or the ways they show and receive love, are often shaped by their culture, the way they were raised, and their own personality. In some cultures, love might be shown through service, while in others, it might be more common to say it out loud. Societal norms and gender roles can also affect how people express themselves, sometimes limiting or directing them in certain ways. Recognizing and accepting these differences is more than just a lesson in tolerance; it's a chance to learn more about love and to find things you have in common with your partner. A holistic point of view recognizes that there are many ways to show love, and that each one is a complex mix of tradition, personality, experience, and emotion.

For Long-term Relationships:

Long-term relationships often depend on both people being able to change and grow, and this includes how love is shown. Over time, a person's love language might change, showing how their life, feelings, or needs have changed. With regular check-ins and honest talk about how love is being shown and felt, both partners can continue to feel valued and understood. Long-term relationships can stay fresh and emotionally satisfying if both people are willing to be flexible in how they show love, try out new ways to show affection and adapt to their partner's changing needs. Also, knowing that a partner's love language might change doesn't make the love less real. Instead, it adds depth and richness to the relationship by showing how love is always changing and has many different sides. Being willing to grow and change in this way could be seen as a sign of love because it shows a commitment to keeping the relationship healthy and happy.

Attachment Styles:

Secure Attachment Style: People who have a secure attachment style usually talk about their love in an open and easy way. In line with Gary Chapman's "Five Love Languages" framework, they might show their love through words, acts of service, quality time, physical touch, or giving gifts. They can also adapt to their partner's preferred love language to ensure their feelings are communicated effectively.

Anxious Attachment Style: People with this style may show their love strongly and often check in with their partner to make sure they feel the same way. They can be very affectionate, spend a lot of time and energy on the relationship, and may show their love through constant communication or reassurances. They might use words of affirmation and quality time a lot as their main ways of showing love.

Avoidant Attachment Style: People with an avoidant attachment style may express love more subtly or indirectly. They might feel more at ease showing their love through acts of service or gifts, which give them some emotional space. They might have trouble showing love in more personal ways, like touching or talking about how they feel.

Disorganized Attachment Style: People with a disorganized attachment style can show love in ways that are not predictable and can go from one extreme to the other. Sometimes they might show a lot of affection and other times they might pull away, just like they did in their past relationships. It can be important for these people and their partners to understand and talk about these patterns.

Question #79:

How do you want to receive love?

Purpose:

The point of this question is to find out how your partner likes to receive love. This is very important if you want your expressions of love to mean something to them and make your relationship better.

Why It's Important:

This enables you to meet your partner's emotional needs effectively, strengthening your connection.

Possible Answers:

- "I feel most loved when I hear words of affirmation."

- "Acts of service make me feel truly cared for."

- "I love receiving thoughtful gifts."

Follow-up Questions:

- Can you share an instance when you felt truly loved? Tell me about a time when you really felt loved.

- What gestures or actions have made you feel unloved or misunderstood in the past?

- Are there ways you'd like me to express love that I haven't yet?

On a Lighter Note:

If they say their preferred love language is receiving gifts and their favorite gifts are puppy snuggles, get ready to be a frequent visitor at your local animal shelter!

Positive and Negative Aspects:

Positive: Knowing how your partner wants to be loved can help you feel closer to them emotionally.

Negative: If their love language is very different from yours, you may have to work harder and understand them better to meet their needs.

Self-Reflection:

How do you most like to be loved? Are you happy with the way your partner shows you love right now?

Practical Guidance:

Talk about your favorite love language and how it makes you feel loved and valued. Is it physical touch, words of encouragement, acts of service, getting gifts, or spending time together? How have you liked to be loved in the past, and are there new ways you might want to try?

Tell them about any problems or obstacles that make it hard for you to accept love. Are there fears or worries from the past that need to be brought up?

Talk about how you can actively tell each other what you need and what you like, especially since these things may change over time or in different situations.

Commit to making an effort to show love in ways that fit with each other's preferences, even if it's outside of your comfort zone. This helps both people feel more connected and happy in the relationship.

Holistic Viewpoints:

Figuring out how you want to be loved is a complicated and nuanced matter that often goes beyond simple likes and dislikes. People's preferred ways to show love are often influenced by a wide range of cultural, social, and personal factors. Some people may have grown up in a family where love was mostly shown through acts of service, while others may have come from a family where love was mostly shown through words. Societal norms and gender stereotypes can also have a big impact, leading people to show or want love in ways that fit with what most people think or expect. The way someone wants to be loved could also reveal more about who they are or what they need emotionally. To build a loving relationship that's both satisfying and respectful, it's important to acknowledge and celebrate these differences. It means being willing to see love not as a single, uniform feeling, but as a deeply personal, culturally rich experience that can be shown and felt in a lot of different ways.

For Long-term Relationships:

In a long-term relationship, figuring out how your partner wants to be loved isn't a one-time thing, but rather a process of learning and changing over time. As people grow and change, their favorite ways to show love may also change to reflect their new interests, values, or ways of seeing themselves and their relationship. With regular check-ins and honest, open communication, both partners can continue to feel loved and appreciated in ways that are meaningful to them. It also encourages flexibility and a sense of wonder, which both partners can use to find new ways to show love and meet each other's changing needs and wants. This dynamic approach to love not only keeps the relationship interesting and new but also strengthens the emotional connection by constantly reminding each other of their shared commitment to the happiness and fulfillment of the other.

Question #80:

What does an ideal romantic relationship look like to you?

Purpose:

This question is meant to find out what your partner wants and expects from a romantic relationship. This will help you figure out if your relationship goals are compatible with theirs.

Why It's Important:

This helps align expectations, leading to better mutual understanding and relationship satisfaction.

Possible Answers:

- "My idea of a good relationship is one where we can talk openly and help each other reach our goals."

- "I want to be in a relationship with someone who makes me laugh, understands me, and wants to go on adventures with me."

Follow-up Questions:

- What are some non-negotiables in a romantic relationship for you?

- Can you think of any real-life or made-up couples who have the relationship you want?

- How do your past relationships compare to this ideal?

On a Lighter Note:

If they say their ideal relationship involves weekly a cappella singing, get ready to bust out your inner Pentatonix!

Positive and Negative Aspects:

Positive: Knowing what your partner's ideal relationship looks like can help you plan what to do and what to expect.

Negative: An ideal that is not realistic can lead to disappointment or stress.

Self-Reflection:

How do you picture the perfect love relationship? How does it align with your partner's vision?

Practical Guidance:

Talk about what you want and what you expect from the relationship. What are the most important things, qualities, or experiences? How do you think we can work through problems and grow together?

Talk about the balance between being independent and being part of a group. How much time do you want to spend together? How will you keep your own interests and identities?

Find out what you want in terms of communication, solving problems, emotional and physical closeness, and sharing responsibilities. How will you build a relationship that meets both of your needs and reflects what you both value?

Recognize that a perfect relationship isn't about being perfect, but about trying to make each other happy and grow. How will you keep the relationship alive and growing over time?

Holistic Viewpoints:

People's ideas of an ideal relationship can be influenced by their cultural background, personal experiences, societal norms, and personal preferences. Be open to diverse perspectives and remember that a healthy relationship may look different for different people. This includes non-traditional or unconventional relationships such as polyamory, open relationships, and more. The key is mutual respect, understanding, and agreement upon the relationship's terms and boundaries. Always ensure communication and consent are paramount, irrespective of the relationship style.

For a better grasp of non-traditional relationships:

- **Polyamorous Relationships:** In a polyamorous relationship, an individual has multiple relationships with the consent of all involved. It's built upon values of communication, honesty, and mutual respect.

- **Open Relationships:** These relationships are characterized by a couple agreeing that they can have sexual relations outside of their relationship. Clear boundaries and rules are often established to ensure everyone involved feels comfortable and secure.

Every relationship style requires clear communication and understanding between all parties involved. So, while discussing your ideal relationship, be sure to also discuss what it means in terms of exclusivity or openness.

For Long-term Relationships:

In long-term relationships, the idea of an "ideal" romantic relationship can be a living, changing idea that changes and grows with the people involved. At different points in life, when we have different experiences, grow as people, and find ourselves in different situations, things that seemed perfect or important at one time may change into something else. To stay on the same page about what an ideal relationship looks like, partners need to talk, think, and understand each other all the time.

This constant conversation is more than just a practical need; it's a deep sign of commitment and closeness. It means that you are willing to talk about each other's hopes and fears, to challenge and support each other's growth, and to rethink the relationship in ways that honor both your own goals and the goals you share with the other person.

Long-term couples can build a strong and satisfying connection that stays alive and meaningful through all the changes and challenges that life may bring. They can do this by regularly talking about what each person's ideal romantic relationship looks like and finding ways to weave those ideas into a shared future.

Attachment Styles:

Secure Attachment Style: People with a secure attachment style tend to think that an ideal relationship is one in which both people respect and trust each other, talk openly, and treat each other equally. They value consistency, dependability, and being able to share interests and help each other grow as people. They may also talk about how important it is to be able to talk about and solve problems in a healthy way.

Anxious Attachment Style: People with this attachment style might think that the best relationship is one in which they are sure their partner loves and cares for them. They might value being close and talking often, and they might want to spend more time together than apart. They may also say that they need their partner to show them love and reassurance often.

Avoidant Attachment Style: People with an avoidant attachment style might say that their ideal relationship is one in which they have a certain amount of freedom and independence. They might value their own space, like to do their own things, and want less emotional involvement. They may also want a partner who understands and respects their need for alone time and their desire for less obvious ways to show affection.

Disorganized Attachment Style: People with a disorganized attachment style may find it hard to describe the perfect relationship because their desire for intimacy and fear of it change over time. Their idea of the perfect relationship could include times when they are very close and times when they are not. They might also talk about how important it is to have a partner who is understanding and patient and can offer stability and support.

Question #81:

What is your view on public displays of affection (PDA)?

Purpose:

This question is meant to find out how comfortable your partner is with showing affection in public. This can affect how you behave as a couple in social situations.

Why It's Important:

Comfort levels with public affection vary widely. Discussing this ensures both partners feel respected and comfortable.

Possible Answers:

- "I am fine with small gestures, like holding hands or giving a quick kiss."

- "I prefer to keep romantic moments private."

Follow-up Questions:

- Do you feel more comfortable with some types of PDA than others?

- Have your opinions on PDA changed over time?

- How would you feel if your partner wanted more or less PDA than you?

On a Lighter Note:

"If they say they want public declarations of love like those viral TikTok couples, you might want to start practicing your dance moves. Don't worry, love in the 21st century just requires a good Wi-Fi connection!"

Positive and Negative Aspects:

Positive: Knowing how each other feels about PDA can help you avoid awkward situations and show each other respect.

Negative: Different levels of comfort may require compromise and talking.

Self-Reflection:

How do you feel about PDA? Are there any particular actions you're comfortable with or not?

Practical Guidance:

Talk about what PDA means to each of you and what actions or words make you feel comfortable or uneasy. Is it when you hold hands, kiss, or hug, or is it something else? How have you handled PDA in the past, and how might you want to handle it in this relationship?

Find out what your values or beliefs are that make you think the way you do about PDA. Are there personal, cultural, or family influences that need to be taken into account?

Talk about how you'll handle PDA in different settings or situations where it might feel more or less appropriate. How will you say what you want or what worries you in the moment?

Set up a plan for how you'll handle PDA in your relationship, taking into account each other's comfort levels and being ready to talk and change as needed.

At the end of the day, this question is about how to make a connection that feels real and respectful, both to each other and to the larger community you live in. By talking openly and carefully, you're laying the groundwork for a relationship that's based on both of your values, needs, and wants.

Holistic Viewpoints:

Public displays of affection (PDA) can be a complicated and multifaceted issue. People's comfort levels can be affected by cultural norms, personal upbringing, societal attitudes, and their own personalities, among other things. For example, PDA might be frowned upon or even forbidden in some cultures, while in others it might be seen as a normal way to show love. How LGBTQ+ couples handle PDA can be complicated because people's reactions can be very different. People also often have very specific and personal feelings about PDA based on their own experiences and levels of comfort. Respecting and understanding each other's preferences can help create a balanced relationship where both people feel comfortable in public.

For Long-term Relationships:

When two people are together for a long time, their feelings about PDA might change over time. This can happen because of personal growth, changes in the social environment, or changes in the way the relationship works. By talking openly and often about how close you want to be, you can avoid misunderstandings and build a relationship that respects both partners' feelings. Being aware of each other's needs and willing to reevaluate and change as the relationship changes can make for a more respectful and fulfilling relationship.

Expert Insight:

When it comes to public displays of affection, people who know a lot about how relationships work stress the importance of clear communication and mutual respect. Dr. Terri Orbuch, a professor at Oakland University and the author of "5 Simple Steps to Take Your Marriage from Good to Great,"[2] says that differences in comfort levels with PDA are often about personal preferences and shouldn't be taken as a sign of how much love or

---

2. Terri Orbuch, "5 Easy Steps to Make Your Good Marriage Great," Harlequin, 2009.

affection is in the relationship. Dr. Orbuch says that couples should talk about how they feel about PDA and try to understand and work with each other's comfort levels instead of trying to change them.

Question #82:

What are some unique or creative date night ideas you'd like to try?

Purpose:

The goal is to find out how adventurous your partner is and what kinds of unique experiences they want to try.

Why it's Important:

Trying new and fun things together is a great way to keep the spark alive in a relationship. By talking about this topic, you can find out what kinds of unique, exciting, or creative things your partner likes to do.

Possible Answers:

- "I've always wanted to try a cooking class together or have a picnic under the stars."

- "Maybe we could create art together, or go on a surprise trip to an undisclosed location."

Follow-Up Questions:

- What makes these date ideas appealing to you?

- How often do you think we should have date nights?

On a Lighter Note:

"How about a romantic evening of competitive taxidermy? Too much? Okay, okay, we can stick to a cooking class then."

Positive and Negative Aspects:

Positive: It could lead to fun, unique date nights that keep the relationship fresh and interesting.

Negative: There could be disagreements or different interests, but this could be a great chance to find a middle ground and try something new.

Self-Reflection:

Think about what kinds of different or creative date nights you would like to have. Would you rather have a quiet, romantic date or an exciting, heart-racing one?

Practical Guidance:

Creative date nights can bring a couple more joy, connection, new experiences, and shared memories.

Talk about how you feel, what you want, or what you value during unique or creative date nights. Focus on newness, joy, connection, or shared experiences as you try to figure out what drives, resonates with, or feeds your connection.

Find out how you and your partner will plan, make, or enjoy creative or unique date nights that will bring you both joy, connection, new experiences, and memories.

Make a "date night jar" with different unique and creative ideas, and pick one out of it every so often to try with your partner.

Holistic Viewpoints:

When planning creative or unique dates, it's important to think about the different preferences, cultural norms, and possible limits of the people involved. Here are some ideas for everyone:

Explore each other's cultures by going to a festival or trying a new dish that comes from one or both of your backgrounds.

Artistic Expression: Take a pottery or painting class that lets you show your creativity.

Accessible Adventures: Plan things to do that are good for people with different levels of physical ability, such as scenic drives, accessible parks, and sports that can be played in different ways.

For Long-term Relationships:

Couples who have been together for a while can rekindle their love by trying new things together:

Memory Lane: Go back to the place of your first date or another important place and think about it.

Take a class together to learn something new, like how to dance or cook a certain type of food.

Looking for an adventure? Plan a weekend trip to a nearby town or nature reserve.

Expert Insight:

Research backs up the idea that doing new and fun things together can make a relationship happier. Some suggestions backed by science are:

Shared Challenges: Do things like an escape room or a cooking challenge that require teamwork.

Hiking, looking at the stars, or having a picnic on the beach are all ways to explore the outdoors together.

Spontaneous Dates: Keep a jar with different ideas for dates, and each week pick one at random for a fun surprise.

Question #83:

What does your ideal date night look like?

Purpose:

This question is meant to find out what your partner likes to do on a romantic date.

Why it's Important:

If you know what your partner's ideal date is, you can plan dates that you and your partner will both enjoy. This can help you have more shared experiences, make good memories, and improve the quality of your relationship as a whole.

Possible Answers:

- "A quiet dinner at home with a movie afterward."

- "Trying out a new restaurant or event in town."

Follow-Up Questions:

- What elements make a date night perfect for you?

- How do you feel about surprise dates?

On a Lighter Note:

"Does binge-watching our favorite series with a giant tub of ice cream count as a date? Yes? Perfect!"

Positive and Negative Aspects:

Positive: You get to understand what makes your partner feel loved and cared for. With this information, you can plan date nights that will be a hit.

Negative: If you and your date have very different ideas of what a perfect date is, it may take some understanding and compromise to plan activities that you both enjoy.

Self-Reflection:

Imagine what your perfect date would be like. Is it a quiet dinner at home, a night out on the town, or an exciting day trip?

Practical Guidance:

Talk about how you feel, what you want, or what you value about your ideal date night. Learn what makes your relationship work by focusing on happiness, intimacy, shared interests, or relaxation.

Find out how you and your partner will plan, make, or enjoy perfect date nights that will bring you both happiness, connection, intimacy, and memories.

Plan and go on each other's ideal date night, and enjoy the chance to learn more about what makes your partner happy and brings you closer to them.

Holistic Viewpoints:

Different people have very different ideas of what a "ideal" date night looks like. Here is what to think about:

Cultural Sensitivity: Depending on cultural norms, a perfect date could include getting together with family, doing something traditional, or going to church.

Personal Interests: If one person likes to do things outside and the other likes to think, combining the two can make for a great date.

Accessibility: Think about mobility or other needs to make sure everyone has a good time on the date.

For Long-term Relationships:

For people who are already in relationships, a perfect date night can be a chance to:

Memories can be brought back to life by going back to places that are special to you.

Trying something new together can add excitement to a relationship.

Simple Pleasures: Sometimes the most romantic date is a night in with a favorite movie, a home-cooked meal, and deep conversation.

Expert Insight:

Research shows that date nights are important for keeping a healthy relationship[3] :

Date nights help couples talk and get closer by giving them a chance to spend time together.

How to Handle Arguments: Spending quality time together can help couples handle arguments better.

Reducing stress: Doing fun things together can make you feel less stressed.

---

3. https://www.prnewswire.com/news-releases/date-nights-linked-to-stronger-marria ges-more-sexual-satisfaction-according-to-new-study-301742711.html#:~:text=For %20couples%20who%20go%20on,%3B%2051%25%20for%20husbands).

CHAPTER FIFTEEN

SEX

EXPLORING DESIRE, INTIMACY, AND SEXUAL HARMONY

Question #84:

How important is physical intimacy to you?

Purpose:

This question is meant to help you figure out what your partner wants and thinks about physical intimacy. It is important for making sure you are both happy and comfortable in the relationship.

Why It's Important:

Physical intimacy plays a crucial role in emotional closeness. Discussing this helps maintain a satisfying romantic relationship.

Possible Answers:

- "Physical intimacy is very important to me. It's one of the ways I feel closest to my partner."

- "I value emotional intimacy more, but physical intimacy has its place."

Follow-up Questions:

- How do you feel when physical intimacy is lacking in a relationship?

- What forms of physical intimacy do you enjoy the most?

- Are there any physical boundaries that you'd like to establish?

On a Lighter Note:

If they say that their preferred form of physical intimacy is a three-legged race, get ready for some fun and occasional falls!

Positive and Negative Aspects:

Positive: Understanding your partner's need for physical intimacy can make your relationship stronger.

Negative: If your needs are different, you may need to be flexible and understand each other.

Self-Reflection:

What role does physical intimacy play in your life? How can you align your needs with your partner's?

Practical Guidance:

Talk about what physical closeness means to you both and why it's important. What are the most important parts of physical intimacy? How do you see the link between being close physically and being close emotionally?

Explore your past experiences, preferences, limits, and any fears or insecurities you might have about being physically close to someone. How will you make sure that the physical part of this relationship is safe and satisfying?

Talk about how you'll handle problems or differences in this area. How will you tell your partner what you want and what you need? How will you make choices that take both your feelings and your values into account?

Holistic Viewpoints:

Physical intimacy can be a complicated and very personal topic. People's tastes, comfort levels, and needs for physical closeness are often shaped by a mix of things, such as their cultural backgrounds, personal experiences, personal preferences, and health. Some people may find connection and happiness through physical intimacy, while others, like those who identify as asexual, may not be interested in sexual activities or have little interest in them. This wide range shows how important it is to approach the topic with sensitivity, understanding, and respect for the unique and often deeply personal factors that shape each person's relationship with physical intimacy.

For Long-term Relationships:

In long-term relationships, keeping physical intimacy in sync can take effort and the ability to change. Levels of physical intimacy might change over time because of things like age, health, life stressors, or changes in the emotional connection between two people. These changes are normal and natural, but they can cause problems if they aren't talked about openly and with care. Regular communication about physical needs and preferences, a willingness to change to meet the other person's changing needs, and a focus on emotional connection and mutual respect can lead to a long-lasting and satisfying physical relationship. Couples can build a strong and responsive connection that helps the health and happiness of their relationship as a whole by thinking of physical intimacy as a conversation that goes on over time instead of a set agreement.

Expert Insight:

According to Dr. Gary Chapman, Physical Touch is one of the five primary love languages. For some people, meaningful touch like hugging, kissing, or sexual intimacy is their primary way of feeling loved and connected. However, the importance of physical intimacy can vary significantly among individuals, and it's vital to understand and respect each other's preferences and boundaries.

Question #85:

Are there any specific boundaries or preferences you have when it comes to our intimate life?

Purpose:

The goal is to talk about each other's needs, limits, preferences, and expectations when it comes to being close in the relationship.

Why It's Important:

Talking about how close you are to each other is important for a healthy and happy relationship. It lets both people feel safe, understood, and respected when it comes to their own needs and wants.

Possible Answers:

- "As part of our closeness, I value emotional connection and communication."

- "I have certain needs or limits that I'd like to talk about in private."

Follow-up Questions:

- What does it mean to you to be close?

- How can we make sure we're talking about our needs and wants in a good way?

- Are there any things you like or don't like because of things that happened in the past?

On a Lighter Note:

They might be a certified Cuddle Expert if they say, "I need at least five minutes of cuddling after every romantic dinner." Get ready to enjoy the cuddles!

Positive and Negative Aspects:

Positive: Open communication builds trust and relationships.

Negative: Misunderstandings or wrong assumptions can make people feel uncomfortable or unhappy.

Self-Reflection:

Think about what intimacy means to you and what your limits or preferences might be. Think about how you can tell your partner about these ideas.

Practical Guidance:

Find a safe, private place to talk about this. Be honest, open, and accepting when you talk about how you feel. Listen to your partner's needs and work with them to make a relationship that works for both of you.

Holistic Viewpoints:

Intimacy isn't just about being close physically; it also involves emotional, mental, and even spiritual connections. The deeper and more satisfying your relationship is likely to be, the more open and honest you can be about these things.

For Long-Term Relationships:

As relationships change, so do personal needs and boundaries. Checking in on this topic often can improve your relationship and make it stronger over time.

Expert Insight – Nurturing Intimacy:

Intimacy is a part of relationships that changes over time and has many different parts. For a relationship to be fulfilling and respectful, both people need to be able to talk openly about their limits and preferences. Couples can create a unique and deeply satisfying life together if they respect each other's differences and work together.

It's a common misconception that the more comfortable you are with someone, the less important it is to maintain healthy boundaries.

They think of limits as a protective mechanism and that they are unnecessary in a close relationship like marriage. Keep in mind the significance of talking about sexual limits at all times. Here are a few examples of sexual boundaries:

- Keeping your private parts to yourself, even when you're with your partner.

- Refusing to do anything that makes you feel uncomfortable, no matter how common that thing might be.

- Not wanting to start sexual contact.

- Refusing to have sexual relations unless both partners use some kind of birth control (usually a condom).

- Not masturbating in front of your partner.

- Keeping your distance from your partner until you're both sure it's safe to get close.

In the end, the goal is to reach an agreement that respects both partners' needs, wants, and limits. This process requires ongoing conversation, empathy, and a commitment to growing together in a very personal way.

Question #86:

What are your expectations regarding sexual intimacy in a marriage?

Purpose:

The goal is to be clear about and understand each other's sexual expectations, beliefs, and desires in marriage.

Why It's Important:

Sexual intimacy can be an important and complicated part of a marriage. By talking about it openly, both partners can make sure they are on the same page, which can lead to more happiness and a stronger bond.

Possible Answers:

- "I think that sexual intimacy is an important part of our relationship, and I like when we do it often."

- "I think that sexual intimacy is a part of our relationship, and I'm open to finding a balance that works for both of us."

Follow-up Questions:

- How do you think our sexual relationship will change as time goes on?

- Do you have any specific needs or limits you'd like to talk about?

- How does talking affect the way we feel about each other?

On a Lighter Note:

If they tell you, "Before every romantic night, I expect a candlelit dinner," you might want to buy additional fire insurance!

Positive and Negative Aspects:

Positive: Understanding what each other wants makes it easier to trust each other and can increase sexual satisfaction.

Negative: Different expectations may lead to misunderstandings or disappointments if they aren't talked about.

Self-Reflection:

Think about what you want and what you need when it comes to sexual intimacy in your marriage. How can you tell your partner these things in a clear way?

Practical Guidance:

Choose a place that is comfortable and private to talk about this sensitive subject. When you share your thoughts, be open, honest, and respectful, and really listen to what your partner has to say. It might be good to talk about this again every so often, since needs and wants can change over time.

Holistic Viewpoints:

Sexual intimacy is just one part of a relationship that includes emotional, intellectual, and spiritual ties. The right amount and value of sexual intimacy may be different for each couple, and that's fine. The most important thing is to find what works best for both people.

For Long-term Relationships:

Sexual intimacy usually grows as a couple gets to know each other better. Changes in life, health, the way a family works, and many other things can affect this. By talking about this topic again and again, you can keep your relationship alive and adapt to each other's changing needs and wants.

Question #87:

How do you envision maintaining a satisfying sexual connection as our relationship evolves?

Purpose:

The goal is to talk about and plan ways to keep and grow a satisfying sexual connection as life changes and challenges come up in the relationship.

Why It's Important:

A good sexual connection can make a relationship more enjoyable overall. Realizing that sexual needs and wants can change over time and making plans to deal with those changes can help make a long-term relationship more satisfying.

Possible Answers:

- "I think that staying in touch and trying out new ways to get close will keep our sexual relationship interesting and fulfilling."

- "I think our relationship will stay strong if we make our closeness a priority and spend time with each other, even when life gets busy."

Follow-up Questions:

- What do you think could change our sexual connection over time, and how can we deal with those changes?

- Are there certain things or ideas you'd like to try to keep our sexual relationship alive?

On a Lighter Note:

If they say, "I'm going to keep a stash of love notes and surprise you when you least expect it," you might want to keep an eye out for hidden surprises in your daily life. A little mystery can add a lot of excitement.

Positive and Negative Aspects:

Positive: Planning how your sexual relationship will change shows that you want to keep this important connection.

Negative: If you don't deal with this part, it might not live up to your expectations or make you less happy over time.

Self-Reflection:

What do you think and feel about how sexual intimacy in your relationship has changed over time? What steps are you willing to take to make things better?

Practical Guidance:

Go out of your way to make time for intimacy. Set aside regular time for each other, be willing to try new things, and talk to each other in an open and honest way. Know that getting sexual satisfaction often takes work, creativity, and the ability to change.

Holistic Viewpoints:

Sexual satisfaction doesn't exist in a vacuum; it's tied to the overall health of the relationship, the emotional connection between the two people, and how well they talk to each other. Taking care of these things will often lead to better sexual intimacy.

For Long-Term Relationships:

Sexual wants and needs can change as a relationship grows. This could be affected by things like becoming a parent, changing jobs, getting sick, or getting older. By talking about sexual connection, being flexible, and taking care of the relationship, this change can be a source of growth rather than conflict.

Expert Insight:

When it comes to keeping a satisfying sexual connection, therapists often stress the importance of regular communication, emotional intimacy, and a willingness to try new things. This ongoing work can help you learn more about each other and enjoy each other more, which will strengthen this important part of your relationship.

A study by Anik Debrot[1] and her colleagues shows that it's not the sex itself that plays the surprising role, but the affection that comes with it between partners. Debrot and her fellow researchers were able to figure out, through a series of four separate studies, how everyday kissing, hugging, and other forms of touch between partners contribute in a unique way to relationship satisfaction and overall well-being.

In short, imagining the future of sexual intimacy in a relationship takes open communication, creativity, flexibility, and a strong desire to keep this important connection. In this close part of life, it's important to realize that both your needs and those of your partner can change.

---

1. Debrot, Anik & Meuwly, Nathalie & Muise, Amy & Impett, Emily & Schoebi, Dominik. (2017). More Than Just Sex: Affection Mediates the Association Between Sexual Activity and Well-Being. Personality and Social Psychology Bulletin. 014616721668412. 10.1177/0146167216684124.

https://greatergood.berkeley.edu/article/item/why_sex_is_so_good_for_your_rel ationship

Question #88:

How comfortable are you discussing sexual topics openly and honestly?

Purpose:

The goal is to find out how comfortable your partner is with openly talking about sexual topics, preferences, and needs, and to find a way to talk that leads to sexual satisfaction and understanding.

Why It's Important:

Talking openly and honestly about sexual matters can greatly improve sexual satisfaction, build trust, and keep misunderstandings from happening in a relationship. To build a supportive and satisfying sexual relationship, it's important to know how each other feels about talking about these things.

Possible Answers:

- "I'm fine talking about anything that has to do with our sexual lives."

- "I may need some time to feel comfortable talking about some things, but I'm willing to work on it."

Follow-up Questions:

- What would make it easier for you to talk about these things?

- Are there certain areas or topics that you find harder to talk about? If so, what are they and how can we talk about them?

On a Lighter Note:

If they say, "I'm an open book, but I blush easily," you might want to keep a blushing emoji handy for text conversations.

Positive and Negative Aspects:

Positive: Talking openly about sexual issues leads to more understanding and happiness.

Negative: If these kinds of talks aren't handled with care and sensitivity, they could make people feel uncomfortable or lead to misunderstandings.

Self-Reflection:

Think about your own level of comfort when talking about sexual topics. What could your partner do to help you have these conversations?

Practical Guidance:

It's a good thing to talk openly about sexual issues, but many people might find it scary. To keep these kinds of conversations going, it's important to pick the right setting. Both people can feel more comfortable in a place that is private and free of distractions. When talking about these things, it's important to show respect and understanding. Using "I" statements can help you talk about how you feel without making the other person feel attacked. On the other hand, "active listening," which means really trying to understand what the other person is saying without judging or interrupting, can make a huge difference. Sometimes, bringing in outside resources like books or advice from a professional can give the conversation structure or a neutral point of view, especially if the topics are hard.

Holistic Viewpoints:

Sexual conversations are about more than just physical preferences. It has a lot to do with how we feel, what we believe, and even what we did in the past. Everyone's level of comfort with these kinds of talks is different. This comfort is often shaped by many things, like how someone was raised, their past relationships, their cultural background, and their own experiences. It's also important to remember that the path to full openness is often a slow one. With trust and patience, a conversation that starts off slow can turn into a deeper, more open, and trusting dialogue over time. At their core, these talks aren't just about the physical act; they're also about the emotional bonds, trust, and closeness that two people share.

For Long-Term Relationships:

A long-term relationship is like a tapestry, with many changes in wants, health, life situations, and feelings. Sexual issues still need to be talked about openly, and this is important. As a couple ages, faces health problems, or goes through events like having a child, being able to talk about intimate things in a comfortable way becomes a key part of staying close. What was true at the start of the relationship may no longer be true, so it's important to talk about these things often to make sure everyone understands and has the same expectations. When sexual topics are hard to talk about or cause fights, couples therapy or counseling can be very helpful. A person who specializes in sexual health can give advice, help guide conversations, and offer insights to help the relationship grow.

Expert Insight:

Research and clinical data[2] show that when a couple has sexual problems, they don't talk about sexual things as much as they should.

Therapists and sex educators often talk about how important it is to have these conversations in a safe, non-judgmental space. Using "I" statements, asking open-ended questions, and stating needs and wants in a positive way are all good ways to communicate.

In the end, figuring out how comfortable you are with talking about sexual topics openly and honestly sets the stage for a satisfying and close sexual relationship. It helps both

---

2. Mallory, Allen B., Stanton, Amelia M., Handy, Ariel B.- (2019) - Couples' sexual communication and dimensions of sexual function: A meta-analysis
https://www.ncbi.nlm.nih.gov/pmc/articles/PMC6699928/

partners understand each other better, builds trust, and can be a source of growth and happiness in the relationship.

Question #89:

Are there any concerns or fears you have related to our sexual compatibility that we should address?

Purpose:

The goal is to get people to talk openly about any worries or fears they have about their sexual compatibility in the relationship so that they can understand them and work on them together.

Why It's Important:

Sexual compatibility has many different parts. It includes physical attraction, preferences, desires, and an emotional bond. Getting to the bottom of any worries early on makes for a better sexual relationship and helps avoid misunderstandings or frustrations.

Possible Answers:

- "I'm worried that our libidos might not be compatible."

- "I worry that we have too many different sexual interests."

Follow-up Questions:

- What specific things about our sexual compatibility worry you?

- How can we talk about what we want and what we like in a way that makes us both feel good?

On a Lighter Note:

If they say, "My only fear is that you won't like my collection of funny underwear," you might laugh and find a new place to shop together.

Positive and Negative Aspects:

Positive: Talking about and addressing worries can make a couple more sexually compatible and build trust.

Negative: If you don't handle this conversation carefully, it could make people feel defensive or anxious.

Self-reflection:

Do you have any worries or fears about how well you and someone else get along sexually? How can you talk about them honestly and with care?

Practical Guidance:

To talk about worries or fears about sexual compatibility, you need to be understanding, open, and not judgmental. Having a planned conversation about sexual compatibility can help both partners feel heard and respected, whether it's about preferences, fears, or misunderstandings. This could mean being clear about your feelings and worries and asking your partner open-ended questions to get to know their point of view. If you need to, you can also get help from a therapist or counselor who specializes in sexual health to have this conversation in a safe and organized way.

Holistic Viewpoints:

Sexual compatibility has to do with more than just how attractive someone is or how a relationship works. It has to do with partners' deeper emotional connections, trust, and ability to understand each other. Concerns or fears can come from a number of places, such as past experiences, beliefs from society or culture, or personal insecurities. To solve these problems, it's not about finding quick fixes, but about getting people to understand

and accept each other better. Understanding that sexual compatibility changes over time, just like other parts of a relationship, and that it can be fostered and grown can help ease some of the fears or pressures that come with this topic.

For Long-term Relationships:

Sexual compatibility doesn't stay the same in long-term relationships. It grows and changes as the relationship matures and as life changes. Open talk about worries or fears about sexual compatibility shouldn't be a one-time thing but should happen often. Being willing to talk about these worries as they come up, knowing that sexual needs and wants can change, and being able to adjust can lead to a more fulfilling and satisfying sexual relationship. Sometimes, these talks can reveal deeper problems that have nothing to do with sexual compatibility but still affect it. The key to a strong sexual connection in a long-term relationship is being willing to talk about these deeper issues.

Expert Insight:

Sexual therapists often say that being sexually compatible isn't just about having the same tastes. It's also about being able and willing to talk, negotiate, and enjoy finding out what each other likes.

In short, addressing worries or fears about sexual compatibility makes for a stronger foundation for a satisfying sexual relationship. It encourages people to work together, understand each other, and go on a journey together to explore and enjoy each other's sexuality. It's a process that deepens closeness and trust, making the connection between the two people stronger.

CHAPTER SIXTEEN

TRUST AND SECURITY

BUILDING A SAFE HAVEN IN EACH OTHER

Question #90:

How important is trust in a relationship for you?

Purpose:

With this question, you can find out how your partner feels about trust, which is one of the most important parts of any relationship.

Why It's Important:

Trust is the foundation of any relationship. Understanding its importance to each partner can ensure its maintenance.

Possible Answers:

- "As important as oxygen for breathing."

- "I can deal with some doubts, but trust is pretty important in general."

Follow-up Questions:

- How do you build trust in a relationship?

- Have you ever had to rebuild trust? How did you handle it?

On a Lighter Note:

"So, are we talking about trust as in 'I trust you to save me the last slice of pizza while I go to the restroom,' or 'I trust you with my Netflix password?' Both are quite serious, you know."

Positive and Negative Aspects:

Positive: A healthy relationship is built on trust. Without it, things can feel shaky in relationships.

Negative: But know that building trust and getting it back takes time and work.

Self-Reflection:

Think about the people you have loved before. Have you been trustworthy? Do you give trust easily?

Practical Guidance:

Talk about how trust in relationships affects your values, beliefs, or experiences. Focusing on honesty, consistency, respect, or shared values can help you figure out what makes trust grow, stays the same, or goes away for each of you.

Think about how you'll build, keep, and restore trust in your relationship. Think about how to create a place where people can trust each other through open communication, mutual respect, and shared commitments. What actions, shared ideas, or honesty might be involved?

Holistic Viewpoints:

Trust is a complicated and very personal thing that can be affected by many things, like a person's background and what they've been through in the past.

Betrayals in the Past: People who have been betrayed in relationships in the past may find it harder to trust again. It's important to be aware of these problems and to deal with them with patience and understanding. To build trust, people may need to talk to each other in a clear, consistent way and do things that show they can be trusted.

Cultural Influences: Different cultures may have different rules and expectations when it comes to trust in relationships. If you understand and respect these differences, you can build a deeper connection.

Personal Values: When it comes to trust, each person may have different values and goals. Partners can make sure that their expectations are the same by talking to each other in an open and caring way.

For Long-term Relationships:

In long-term relationships, trust is not a fixed trait, but something that changes over time and needs constant care.

Trust isn't just built at the beginning of a relationship; it needs to be kept up and cared for all the time. This process may include regular check-ins, honest communication, and actions that show commitment and dependability over and over again.

Challenges can come up in long-term relationships, and they can test trust. How a couple deals with these problems can make or break their trust in each other. During hard times, trust can be built by being proactive, honest, and helpful.

Expert Insight:

Relationship experts[1] can give us valuable information about how trust works.

Rebuilding Trust: Both parties need to do and think certain things to rebuild trust after a breach. The person who broke trust must be honest, consistent, and patient, and the person whose trust was broken must be willing to take risks and be vulnerable again. Both partners have to learn and practice new steps together to do this complicated "dance."

Trust as a Base: Many relationship experts say that trust is the most important part of any good relationship. Without trust, it's hard to keep other important parts of a relationship going, like closeness, connection, and working together.

---

1. https://www.healthymarriageinfo.org/wp-content/uploads/2017/12/Why-Trust-Matters-in-Relationships.pdf

Question #91:

What makes you feel secure in a relationship?

Purpose:

This question is meant to help you find out what your partner's emotional needs are and what makes them feel safe and loved.

Why It's Important:

Security in a relationship is key to emotional well-being. Knowing what provides that sense of security can guide actions and behaviors within the relationship.

Possible Answers:

- "Knowing that we can talk about anything openly and honestly."

- "Having a close relationship based on trust and respect."

Follow-up Questions:

- Can you provide specific examples?

- How do you say that you want to feel safe?

On a Lighter Note:

"Is a fortress of pillows enough security or should we opt for the moat with sharks?"

Positive and Negative Aspects:

Positive: Happiness can come from feeling safe,

Negative: ut a strong need for safety could be a sign of dependency issues.

Self-Reflection:

What makes you feel safe in a relationship? Are you willing and able to give your partner what they need to feel safe?

Practical Guidance:

In a relationship, security often comes from a complex mix of trust, connection, understanding, and having the same values.

Talk about what your needs, expectations, behaviors, or experiences are that make you feel safe in a relationship. Figure out how your sense of security is affected by your personality, past relationships, or personal values.

Think about how you will create, recognize, and maintain safety in your relationship. Think about ways to build a stable, supportive, and connected relationship that fits both your needs and your values. What actions, ideas, or feelings of empathy might be involved?

Holistic Viewpoints:

How safe someone feels in a relationship often depends on their likes, needs, and experiences. Here are some key things to think about:

Personal Needs and Expectations: Different people may have different ideas about what makes them feel safe and what they need to feel safe. Some people may need frequent reassurances and quality time, while others may value acts of service or commitment to shared goals.

Past Experiences: A person's need for security in a relationship can be shaped by their past, especially if they've been through something traumatic. Someone who has been betrayed in the past might need more clear and consistent promises of loyalty and honesty.

Style of Communication: Open, honest, and caring communication is often key to feeling safe. It helps people understand each other's needs and act in a way that meets those needs.

Emotional Availability: Responding to your partner's feelings and needs can give them a sense of security. Being open emotionally helps build trust and connection.

For Long-term Relationships:

Long-term relationships have their own unique dynamics and security concerns:

Changing Needs: Over time, people change, and their needs and preferences can also change. Continuous assessment and communication make sure that the security needs are met as the relationship grows.

Maintaining intimacy: In long-term relationships, it takes work to keep things close. When you feel safe in a relationship, it makes it easier to be vulnerable and real.

Facing Life Changes Together: Changes and challenges in life can either make you feel less safe or more secure. How a couple handles these changes together can have a lasting effect on how stable their relationship is.

Respect and Understanding: When people respect each other's freedom and understand each other's values, beliefs, and life goals, they feel safer. It reinforces the idea that both people are in the relationship voluntarily and like each other's unique qualities.

Expert Insight – Attachment Styles:

Secure Attachment Style: People who have a secure attachment style are usually warm and loving and don't mind being close to others. They also know how to set limits and don't worry much about their relationships.

Anxious Attachment Style: People who are anxious often think a lot about their relationships and worry about whether or not their partner can love them back. They often need to be reassured and validated often.

Avoidant Attachment Style: People with an avoidant attachment style think that being close to someone means losing their independence, so they try to stay as far away from each other as possible. They push their partners away and try to hide how they feel.

Disorganized Attachment Style: People with fearful-avoidant attachment, also called "disorganized attachment," have mixed feelings about close relationships. They both want and don't want to be emotionally close. They don't trust their partners and think they aren't good enough.

Question #92:

Have you ever cheated in a relationship?

Purpose:

To find out about the person's past relationships and how honest they are. This question also shows how they feel about commitment and loyalty.

Why it's Important:

Trust and loyalty are the most important parts of a strong relationship. Understanding each other's past actions can help start a conversation about what each person expects from the other in terms of loyalty and commitment.

Possible Answers:

- "No, I value trust and honesty too much to betray my partner."

- "Yes, I made a mistake in the past, but I have learned and grown from that experience."

Follow-Up Questions:

- How has this experience influenced your views on fidelity?

- What have you learned from that experience?

On a Lighter Note:

"Honey, if I cheated on my diet more than I've cheated in any relationship, does that count as a yes?"

Positive and Negative Aspects:

Positive: It allows for openness and honesty and gives people a chance to talk about and learn from past mistakes.

Negative: It might bring up bad feelings and hurts from the past. If you do not handle it carefully, it could hurt the trust and closeness between you and your partner.

Self-Reflection:

Think about your own past and how you feel about cheating now. What made you do these things or would make you do them? How did your relationships change because of it? Reflecting on your own actions can help you understand how your partner feels and talk about ways to stop it from happening again.

Practical Guidance:

Talking about past cheating can be a very personal, sensitive, and difficult conversation that shows trust, honesty, self-awareness, and the values of the relationship.

Focus on context, motivations, regrets, or growth as you think about your past experiences, feelings, or lessons about cheating. Figure out how your values, expectations, or actions in the relationship may have changed because of past cheating.

Talk about how you will handle, deal with, or stop infidelity in your relationship. Think about ways to create a place where honesty, trust, open communication, and shared values are valued. What kinds of agreements, understandings, or limits might be needed?

Holistic Viewpoints:

The question of cheating can be hard to answer, and its effects on different types of relationships can be very different:

Understanding What Cheating Means: Cheating isn't always defined the same way in every relationship. In a monogamous relationship, it usually means breaking trust or breaking a promise. In a non-monogamous relationship, it can mean something different. It could mean breaking rules or limits that both people have agreed to.

Creating a Safe Space: If this subject comes up in conversation, make sure it is talked about with care, compassion, and an open mind. Accusations and assumptions can hurt people and make it hard to talk to them.

Recognizing Complexity: There can be a lot of reasons why people cheat. It could be because they aren't happy with themselves, their needs aren't being met, or they don't understand the commitments that come with being in a relationship.

For Long-term Relationships:

When it comes to long-term relationships, the answer to this question changes:

Even if the cheating is over, talking about it openly can remind both people how important trust, honesty, and loyalty are in the relationship.

Shared Values and Expectations: Talking openly about fidelity helps make sure that the values and expectations of both people are the same.

Learning from the Past: Being aware of past actions and mistakes can help you grow, reaffirm your commitment, and make the relationship stronger.

Expert Insight:

Researchers and relationship experts have important things to say about this topic:

Statistically, people who have cheated in the past are more likely to cheat in future relationships, according to research[2]. People can grow and change, so this doesn't mean it has to happen.

Importance of Communication: Talking openly and honestly about expectations and limits for faithfulness can help prevent misunderstandings and keep trust.

---

2. https://www.ncbi.nlm.nih.gov/pmc/articles/PMC5709195/

Healing and Growth: If someone has cheated, getting help from a professional might help them figure out what went wrong and move toward healing and growth.

Question #93:

Is there anything from your past that I should know about?

Purpose:

To find out about any experiences, events, or situations from the past that might affect the relationship.

Why it's Important:

Everyone has a past, and sometimes parts of that past can change how people interact now and in the future. By being aware of these, you can help your partner understand and care about you more.

Possible Answers:

- "I believe in transparency, so I've shared everything that I feel could impact our relationship."

- "There are some aspects of my past that I'm not proud of, but I've learned and grown from those experiences."

Follow-Up Questions:

- How have these experiences shaped you?

- What lessons have you learned from these experiences?

On a Lighter Note:

"Before we get deep into our past, can we agree that our teenage fashion choices are off-limits for judgment?"

Positive and Negative Aspects:

Positive: This conversation can help partners be more open, trust each other, and understand each other better.

Negative: Thinking about the past might bring up hard feelings or make you feel bad.

Self-Reflection:

Think about your own past and what parts of it you would be comfortable telling your partner.

Practical Guidance:

Talk about how you feel, what you value, or what you think about sharing past experiences. Focus on trust, understanding, vulnerability, or acceptance as you try to figure out what makes you want or need to talk about your past.

Find out how you and your partner will handle, help, or respect this part of sharing in your relationship. This process needs trust, empathy, understanding, and not passing judgment on each other.

Exercise: As a way to build trust, try telling each other a story from your past. This will help you get to know each other better and feel more empathy.

Holistic Viewpoints:

To understand a partner's past, it's important to look into many different things, such as their cultural upbringing, socioeconomic background, health history, family dynamics, and even past traumas. These parts of a person's life may affect what they believe, what they value, how they act, and how they feel. When talking about these topics, you need to be careful, have empathy, and be aware that the information might be sensitive.

Communication that is respectful and kind creates a safe space where partners feel comfortable talking about their pasts

For Long-term Relationships:

People who have been together for a long time often know a lot about each other's pasts. But some areas may not be explored or shared because they were missed or because they were kept secret on purpose. By constantly working to create a trusting and nonjudgmental space, partners can feel safe talking about more personal or hard parts of their pasts. This kind of sharing can deepen emotional closeness and make connections stronger.

Expert Insight:

Studies, like the one done by Alea and Vick[3], show that knowing and understanding your partner's past experiences can make your relationship happier and more stable. It helps people feel more empathy, compassion, and connection. But it's important to know how the different types of attachment can affect this process:

Secure Attachment Style: People with this attachment style are usually open and don't mind talking about their past, which makes it easier to understand each other.

Anxious Attachment Style: People with this style may feel a strong need to talk about their past, but they may also be afraid of being rejected or judged. They may need extra reassurance and understanding.

Avoidant Attachment Style: People with this style may not want to talk about their past because they value independence and privacy. Trust and gradual sharing can grow with patience and gentle encouragement.

Disorganized Attachment Style: This style of attachment could lead to inconsistent or confusing ways of talking about personal history, which could be a sign of fears or

---

3. Alea, N., & Vick, S. C. (2010). The first sight of love: Relationship-defining memories and marital satisfaction across adulthood

trauma that hasn't been dealt with. To deal with this complicated situation, you may need sensitivity and/or help from a professional.

Question #94

How do you feel about maintaining friendships with ex-partners?

Purpose:

This question is meant to find out how your partner feels about keeping in touch with ex-lovers and how comfortable they are with you doing the same.

Why it's important:

Figuring out how to be friends with an ex can be hard and emotional. Knowing where your partner is coming from can help you set limits and expectations.

Possible Answers:

- "I believe it's possible to maintain a healthy friendship with an ex, as long as it's respectful to our relationship."

- "I prefer to not maintain close friendships with exes to avoid complications in my current relationship."

Follow-up Questions:

- Have you maintained friendships with ex-partners in the past?

- How do you navigate boundaries in these friendships?

On a Lighter Note:

Sure, we can be friends with our exes, as long as they don't try to bring up the 'remember when' stories at dinner parties!"

Positive and negative aspects:

Positive: If your partner is okay with keeping in touch with their ex-partners, it could mean that they have healthy closure and can handle complex emotional relationships.

Negative: If your partner does not like it, it could be a sign of unresolved problems or jealousy. If you are still friends with your ex-partners, this could make it harder for you to hang out with other people.

Self-Reflection:

Think about how you feel about staying in touch with your ex-partners. How would it make you feel if your partner had these kinds of friends? Understanding your own level of comfort can help guide the conversation.

Practical Guidance:

This topic could bring up questions about trust, comfort, and personal limits.

Be honest about how you feel about keeping these friendships going. Remember that this is a matter of personal taste, which can vary a lot from person to person.

Exercise: Make an agreement on being friends with ex-partners that spells out the rules and expectations in this area. Make sure that this agreement takes into account both people's feelings and levels of comfort and that it is looked at again as the relationship changes.

Holistic Viewpoints:

Different people may feel very differently about staying friends with their ex-partners in different situations.

From a cultural point of view, some cultures might think it's normal and fine to be friends with an ex, while others might think it's weird. Understanding the cultural background can help you deal with these relationships, which can be complicated.

Personal Beliefs: Each person's morals, values, and past experiences can also have a big impact on how they feel about this issue. It's important to talk openly about personal limits.

For Long-term Relationships:

Long-term relationships can change the way people interact with their ex-partners, which can be tricky to deal with.

Emotional Shift: As emotional ties to an ex-partner weaken over time, the chance of becoming friends may grow. This change should be talked about with the person you're with now.

Clear Boundaries: Both people in a long-term relationship need to feel safe and agree on the nature and limits of their friendships with their ex-partners.

Expert Insight - Attachment Styles:

Several relationship experts give advice on this sensitive subject.

Setting Boundaries: Many experts say that clear boundaries and honest communication are important if you want to stay friends with an ex.

Possible Pitfalls: Some people warn of the possible problems and misunderstandings that could happen and suggest moving forward with care and mutual agreement.

Attachment styles:

Your reaction to staying friends with an ex-partner can depend on your attachment style.

Secure Attachment Style: People who usually trust their partners and talk openly with them might feel more at ease with this idea.

Anxious Attachment Style: People with anxious attachment may find the idea more difficult because they often need constant reassurance and may feel threatened by their partner's connections to exes.

Avoidant Attachment Style: People with this style of attachment may prefer to stay away from their exes, which is in line with how they feel about emotional closeness in general.

Disorganized Attachment Style: Because they have different feelings and wants, people with disorganized attachment may not know how to answer this question. They may go back and forth between wanting to stay connected and being afraid of it.

CHAPTER SEVENTEEN

MONEY AND FINANCES

A PRACTICAL APPROACH TO SHARED FINANCIAL RESPONSIBILITY

Question #95:

How do you feel about spending and saving?

Purpose:

This question helps you figure out how your partner handles money and how they feel about it. Getting to know how they spend and save money can tell you a lot about their financial discipline and priorities.

Why It's Important:

A person's spending and saving habits can greatly affect a couple's financial stability. Understanding these habits can prevent future disagreements.

Possible Answers:

- "I save a lot of my money, but every once in a while, I buy something nice for myself."

- "I tend to spend more than I save, but I am trying to change that."

- "I am a cheap person who puts saving money for the future first."

Follow-up Questions:

- How do you balance your spending and saving?

- What do you spend your money on most of the time?

- How do you choose what to put money away for?

On a Lighter Note:

If they are a spender because they have been saving up to buy the world's largest rubber duck collection, at least you will always have a squeaky friend for bath time!

Positive and Negative Aspects:

Positive: Being a saver could be a sign of financial responsibility and long-term planning, but being too cheap could keep you from doing things.

Negative: On the other hand, being a spender might show that you enjoy life and want to be comfortable, but spending too much can make your finances unstable.

Self-Reflection:

How do you decide how much to spend and how much to save? Is there a balance, or do you tend more toward one side? How do your habits match or differ from those of your partner?

Practical Guidance:

Start by talking about your own ideas about how to spend and save money. Do you like to save as much as possible for the future? Or do you prefer to live in the moment and spend money on things and experiences that make life fun? There is no "right" or "wrong" answer, but your habits and attitudes should match or go together.

Talk about how you spend your money and what it says about your values and priorities. Do you put more value on luxury items, travel, hobbies, or something else? How do these fit into your bigger financial goals and duties?

In the same way, look at how you save money. Why are you saving, and what are you saving for? How do you find a balance between wanting to save money and wanting to live and enjoy life right now? Understanding these dynamics can help people find areas where they agree or where they might disagree.

Consider making a plan for spending and saving that takes into account both of your points of view. This could mean setting shared financial goals, making budgets, or setting spending limits that give everyone freedom but still hold everyone accountable.

Keep in mind that how you feel about money and how you spend it can be very personal and sometimes very emotional. Bring empathy, curiosity, and a willingness to learn from each other to this conversation.

Holistic Viewpoints:

Learning how you spend and save is a journey that goes beyond just managing your money. It talks about cultural influences, upbringing, personal experiences, and income levels, which shows how complicated life is. People have many different ways of spending and saving money, which can be a source of conflict in a relationship. What might look like simple numbers on a balance sheet are actually symbols of more important personal goals and values. To deal with these differences, you need more than just a willingness to compromise. You need empathy, understanding, and a shared vision of what financial stability looks like. By being aware of these complexities and working together to solve them, partners can build a financial partnership that respects each person's uniqueness and helps both of them grow.

For Long-term Relationships:

In a long-term relationship, spending and saving the same amount of money is very important. When money gets mixed up, so do the values and priorities that guide it. Spending and saving money together isn't just about making a budget; it's also a sign of shared goals, responsibilities, and trust. Couples can work through the ups and downs of their finances together if they talk about it and talk about it often. Whether you're planning a trip or putting money away for a rainy day, these conversations are the foundation of a financially healthy relationship. They turn potential disagreements into chances for each person to learn and grow.

Expert Insight:

Finding the right balance between spending and saving is a complicated dance that financial experts have been thinking about for a long time. Dave Ramsey[1] and other well-known financial advisors stress how important it is to enjoy life's pleasures while also planning for the future. When two people get together, they often have different ideas about how much they should spend and how much they should save. Experts like Ramsey say that the key is not to find a perfect match but to find a way to get along with each other. By talking openly, understanding each other's needs and values, and working together to find a balance, couples can create a financial partnership that supports not only their future security but also their happiness and fulfillment in the present.

---

1. Ramsey, D. (2003). The Total Money Makeover: A Proven Plan for Financial Fitness. Thomas Nelson. ISBN 978-0-7852-8908-1.

Question #96:

Do you believe in having a joint account?

Purpose:

This question gets to the heart of what your partner thinks about sharing financial responsibilities and being honest about money. Their answer can show how much they trust you, how financially independent they feel, and how they think you should handle money as a couple.

Why It's Important:

This question brings up financial trust and shared responsibility. It helps couples make joint decisions about money management.

Possible Answers:

- "Yes, I think it is a good way to deal with shared costs."

- "I would rather keep our money separate so that we can be on our own."

- "I am okay with a mix of joint and separate accounts."

Follow-up Questions:

- If you like the idea of a joint account, what kinds of costs do you think it could cover?

- If you're against it, what are your main concerns?

- How would you feel about a joint savings account for shared goals?

On a Lighter Note:

If they do not want a joint account because they are saving up for a Batmobile in secret, you cannot say much against them, can you? Who wouldn't want a ride in that?

Positive and Negative Aspects:

Positive: By choosing a joint account, you could show your commitment to shared financial goals and your willingness to be open.

Negative: If you want separate accounts, it could mean that you want to be financially independent or that you are worried about money fights.

Self-Reflection:

What do you think about shared accounts? Are you and your partner on the same page about this, or do you need to find a middle ground or talk about it more?

Practical Guidance:

Find out why you might want a joint account to start. Many couples find that having a joint account makes it easier to split costs like rent or mortgage payments, utilities, groceries, and other household costs. They could also mean that the couple is more committed to the relationship and trusts each other more.

Not everyone will be happy with this arrangement, though. Some people may want to keep separate accounts so they can feel like they have control over their money. They might be worried about what will happen if the relationship ends or if one person is careless with money.

When you talk about this, make sure to address each other's worries and hopes. What will be done with the joint account? How will people know how much to give? Will there be rules or limits about how much you can spend? What do you do if one of you makes a lot more money than the other?

If you decide to have a joint account, talk about whether you'll still keep separate accounts for your own expenses and savings. Some couples find that a "yours, mine, and ours" approach strikes a good balance between sharing financial responsibilities and respecting each person's independence.

No matter what you decide, the most important thing is that both of you are happy with the arrangement and that it fits with your shared values and goals. Be ready to change your mind about this choice as your relationship changes and your financial needs change.

If you have specific worries or questions about your finances, you might also want to talk to a professional. A financial planner or counselor can give you advice that is unique to you and your partner's financial situations.

Holistic Viewpoints:

Whether someone chooses to keep their finances separate, open joint accounts, or do a mix of the two can depend a lot on their past experiences, cultural background, and personal values about money and independence. Some people may need to be financially independent and keep separate accounts because of how they were raised or what they have been through. For others, a joint account could show that two people are united, trust each other, and have the same financial goals. Some people may also like a mix, with separate accounts for personal costs and a joint account for costs that everyone pays for. It is important to talk about this subject with an open mind and sensitivity and to remember that different ways of handling money can work for different couples. There is no right or wrong here, as long as both people are happy and decisions about money are made with mutual understanding and agreement.

For Long-term Relationships:

When a couple has been together for a long time, they may have different financial needs and goals than when they first met. For example, you might need a joint account now to handle shared costs like the mortgage, the kids' schooling, or shared fun activities. Individual accounts, on the other hand, can be used to save money or spend money for personal goals. Review your shared financial system often and be willing to make changes as needed.

Question #97:

What are your financial goals?

Purpose:

This question is meant to help you learn about your partner's values, priorities, and ability to plan for the future by learning about their financial goals. You can use their answer to figure out how their financial future compares to yours.

Why It's Important:

Financial goals reflect a person's life goals and future plans. Knowing this will help couples make cooperative financial plans.

Possible Answers:

- "I want to save up for a house in the next five years."

- "I want to save money for emergencies and pay off my student loans."

- "I want to retire early so I can travel around the world."

Follow-up Questions:

- How do you plan to get to your financial goals?

- How do you prioritize your financial goals?

- How flexible are you with your goals if things change?

On a Lighter Note:

If their goal with money is to buy enough chocolate to last them a lifetime, then you have found a keeper. (Just remember to balance it out with a lifetime gym membership.)

Positive and Negative Aspects:

Positive: Having clear financial goals shows foresight and financial responsibility.

Negative: Goals that are not realistic or that cannot be changed could cause stress or disappointment.

Self-Reflection:

What are your financial goals? How well do they match the goals of your partner? Can you work together to reach these goals?

Practical Guidance:

First, you might want to write down your own financial goals. These could be short-term goals, like saving for a vacation or paying off a credit card, or long-term goals, like building an investment portfolio or starting a retirement fund. The goals of each person will be based on their values, hopes, and current financial situation.

Once you've written down your own goals, think about how they match or don't match those of your partner. Do you both want to reach the same goals? How can you make things right if there are differences? This could mean putting some goals ahead of others or finding a middle ground that meets the needs and wants of both partners.

Talk about how you plan to reach these goals as well. What are the steps you'll take, how long they'll take, and the strategies you'll use? How will you keep track of your progress and make changes when necessary? This is where working together, being open, and being flexible come into play.

You might also find it helpful to talk to a financial planner, who can give you expert advice that fits your specific needs. Professional help can give you valuable insight and help you make a plan that is realistic and doable.

Holistic Viewpoints:

Our financial goals are often based on what we have done, what we have learned, and how well off we are. Some people may want to own their own home, while others may want to travel or get a better education. Even if their goals are different from yours, it is important to respect and support them. A flexible and caring approach can help couples work through their differences and build a shared financial future that takes into account the goals of both partners.

Question #98:

Do you have any outstanding debt?

Purpose:

This question starts a conversation about financial responsibilities and how they could cause stress. It is important to find out how open your partner is about their finances.

Why It's Important:

Debt can impact future financial plans. Discussing it openly helps maintain financial transparency.

Possible Answers:

- "Yes, I am paying off student loans right now."

- "I am trying to pay off the debt on my credit cards."

- "No, I do not have any debt."

Follow-up Questions:

- What kind of debt is it? (Credit card, student loan, mortgage, etc.)

- How do you plan to pay back this debt?

- How does this debt affect what you want to do with your money?

On a Lighter Note:

If they owe money because they bought all the seasons of "Friends" on Blu-ray, then at least you know they have a good sense of humor, nostalgia, and maybe an unhealthy obsession with sitcoms from the '90s.

Positive and Negative Aspects:

Positive: If the debt is taken on and paid off in a responsible manner, it can serve as a useful tool. It may even be indicative of a readiness to make long-term investments (in things like a child's education or a home).

Negative: However, if you have a lot of debt that you cannot seem to pay off, that could be a sign that you have money problems or bad spending habits.

Self-Reflection:

Where do you stand on debt? How about you? Do you have any? What would you do if you found out that a potential partner was deeply in debt?

Practical Guidance:

Start by telling them about your debts, like credit cards, student loans, mortgages, or personal loans. What are the amounts, rates of interest, and terms for paying back the loans? How does this debt fit into the bigger picture of your finances?

You should also think about why you have debt and what it means to you. Some people might need to take on debt in order to pay for college or a house. For others, it could be a source of stress or a sign that they are not taking care of their money well.

Understanding each other's thoughts and actions about debt can help people talk to each other in a more understanding and helpful way. For example, if one partner doesn't like taking on debt and the other doesn't mind it, this could point to deeper values or fears that need to be addressed.

Talk about how you both plan to deal with debt. Will you work on it together or do it on your own? What methods will you use to pay it off? This could mean making a budget, moving money around, or getting help from a financial counselor.

Being honest about debt is about more than just the numbers; it's also about building trust, showing responsibility, and fostering a shared financial vision.

Holistic Viewpoints:

People's financial situations can be very different, depending on a lot of different things. Debt is not always a red flag; it could be because of student loans, a mortgage, or hard times in the past. When you look at this question, it is important not to judge. Instead, you should try to figure out how your partner is handling their debt and how they plan to pay it off. In some cultures, getting into debt is seen as a sign of being irresponsible, while in others, it is seen as a way to invest in yourself or your future. Respect the fact that your partner's cultural background, personal values, and life experiences may give them different ideas about how to handle debt. When talking about such personal and possibly sensitive topics, it is important to create an atmosphere of understanding and kindness.

For Long-term Relationships:

In a long-term relationship, things like debt are more than just a personal matter; they become a shared responsibility that can have a big effect on the plans and goals of both people. Talking about your partner's debt isn't just practical; it's also a way to build trust and be honest. Your partner's debt could affect big financial steps like buying a house, saving for retirement, or just making a budget. By talking openly and often about how to handle this debt together, you and your partner can come up with a plan that fits with your shared financial goals. It shows how important it is to help and understand each other when building a future together.

Expert Insight:

Financial harmony is often a key part of a stable relationship. Experts like Suze Orman[2] have always said that being honest about debts in a relationship is very important. Orman says that knowing each other's financial obligations, how they handle debt, and even

---

2. Orman, S. (2010). The Money Class: Learn to Create Your New American Dream. Spiegel & Grau. ISBN 978-1-4000-6961-0.

working together to pay it off can strengthen the foundation of a relationship. It's not just about numbers; it's about building trust and a shared commitment to a stable financial future. This kind of open communication is very important for setting realistic goals and avoiding unexpected financial problems in the future.

CHAPTER EIGHTEEN

HOBBIES AND INTERESTS

CELEBRATING INDIVIDUALITY AND SHARED PASSIONS

Question #99:

What is one hobby or interest you'd like to pursue together?

Purpose:

This question is all about finding out if you have similar interests and figuring out if you would work well together on a project. Whether it is rock climbing or crocheting, doing the same things together can make your relationship stronger.

Why It's Important:

Shared hobbies can enhance bonding and enjoyment. Discussing this helps foster mutual interests and shared experiences.

Possible Answers:

- "I've always wanted to take up salsa dancing. It sounds like a fun, spicy way to break a sweat!"

- "Let's create a podcast about the hilarious aspects of everyday life."

Follow-up Questions:

- What makes this hobby interesting to you?

- Are you willing to try new things that I want to do?

- How often do you think we will do this activity?

On a Lighter Note:

If they say, "How about competitive dog grooming? We don't have a dog, but we could borrow one!", you've got a keeper who knows how to keep things light and playful.

Positive and Negative Aspects:

Positive: Shared hobbies can lead to shared experiences that bring people closer together.

Negative: Keep in mind that people may be competitive or have different ideas about how to enjoy the hobby.

Self-Reflection:

Think about what you like to do and what you enjoy. Are you willing to talk about them and learn more about your partner's interests?

Practical Guidance:

Talk about what activities or hobbies you both might enjoy or be interested in trying out together. It could be something new for both of them or something that one of them already likes and wants to share with the other.

Think about how doing a hobby together fits with your shared goals, values, or way of life. How will it make your relationship stronger, give you more things to do together, or help you both grow and be happy?

Think about things like time, money, and commitments when deciding on a hobby to do together. How will you schedule, prioritize, and fit this activity into your daily lives?

Holistic Viewpoints:

Hobbies and interests are very personal and can be very different from one person to the next. Finding things you have in common or sharing each other's interests might take time and understanding. Even if a hobby seems strange or new, if you approach it with curiosity and respect, it can lead to new ways to connect with people and grow.

For Long-term Relationships:

As people get to know each other and grow, their interests may change or they may become interested in something new. The key is to be open and able to change. Trying new things together can keep your relationship interesting and give you chances to learn and laugh with each other. Whether it's something unusual like a dog grooming competition or something common like hiking, doing something together can be rewarding.

Expert Insight:

Experts on relationships often talk about how important it is to do things and have hobbies together. When couples find things they have in common or are willing to try new things together, they are happier and feel closer to each other. It's not just about doing the activity; it's also about spending time together, making memories, and often learning new things about each other. It's a fun and interesting way to learn and grow together. Having a shared interest can be a good thing for any relationship, whether it's a sport, a creative hobby, or something completely different.

Question #100:

Are you okay with me having my own hobbies and interests?

Purpose:

This question is meant to help you figure out how your partner feels about your individuality in a relationship and how well they can respect and support your independence.

Why It's Important:

This question reflects one's views on personal space and individuality within a relationship, crucial for maintaining a healthy balance of togetherness and autonomy.

Possible Answers:

- "Absolutely, I think it's important for each of us to have our own interests."

- "As long as your hobby isn't collecting tarantulas, I think we're good."

Follow-up Questions:

- Would you like to learn about my hobbies, or would you prefer to keep them separate?

- Do you have any concerns about any specific hobbies I might have?

On a Lighter Note:

If they say, "Only if your hobby isn't 'critiquing my cooking skills'," you might need to find a different outlet for your culinary critiques.

Positive and Negative Aspects:

Positive: A partner who respects your personal interests knows how important personal space and independence are, which is a good sign.

Negative: If they seem unwilling or possessive, it could mean they have control or jealousy issues.

Self-Reflection:

Think about how you would feel if your partner did not like your hobbies. Would you give in, try to find a middle ground, or stand your ground?

Practical Guidance:

Talk about your own hobbies and interests and what they mean to you. How do they show your needs, joys, or growth as a person?

Find out how you feel about each other's separate goals. What needs to be set up in terms of trust, limits, or understanding? How will you talk about, negotiate, or deal with these things?

Think about how each person's hobbies or interests fit with the values, goals, or lifestyle choices that you and your partner share. How will they help or hurt your connection, how you manage your time, or the experiences you share?

This conversation helps you and your partner understand each other, trust each other, and respect each other's space and passions. It also strengthens your connection, boundaries, and mutual support.

Expert Insight – Attachment Styles:

Secure Attachment Style: People with a secure attachment style are usually confident and understanding of their partner's need for independence and personal interests. They usually support their partner's hobbies and know how important it is for each person to keep their own identity in a relationship.

Anxious Attachment Style: People with this style may feel insecure or worried when their partner spends time on personal hobbies, especially if it means they spend less time together. They might want to know that their partner's individual interests don't mean they don't care about the relationship or love them.

Avoidant Attachment Style: People with an avoidant attachment style usually like having their own space and don't mind if their partner has their own interests. But they might have trouble if their partner's hobbies take up a lot of time, because it might feel like an invasion of their own space or time.

Disorganized Attachment Style: People with a disorganized attachment style might react differently to their partner's separate interests. They might feel alone sometimes, but at other times, they might like the space. These different answers can make the relationship more confusing and lead to misunderstandings.

Question #101:

Are there any hobbies or interests of mine that you might find difficult to support?

Purpose:

This question is a good way to find out how comfortable your partner is with your interests and hobbies, especially if they are different from their own.

Why It's Important:

It can reveal potential sources of conflict and encourages negotiation and compromise on shared and individual activities.

Possible Answers:

- "I'm okay with most hobbies, but if you decide to breed snakes in our apartment, we may need to have a talk."

- "As long as your hobby doesn't involve us going bankrupt, I'm supportive."

Follow-up Questions:

- Why would you find it difficult to support that particular hobby?

- Is there a way we can reach a compromise on this issue?

On a Lighter Note:

If they say, "If your hobby involves making sculptures from our unused cutlery, we might need to have a chat." You may need to reconsider your kitchen art installations.

Positive and Negative Aspects:

Positive: When people are willing to talk about this topic and find a middle ground, it shows that they respect each other.

Negative: If they dismiss your interests without consideration, it may suggest a lack of empathy or understanding.

Self-Reflection:

How would you feel if your partner did not like your hobbies? Consider potential compromises or solutions.

Practical Guidance:

Find out if either of you has any hobbies or interests that might worry or challenge the other person. Why might it be hard to help them? What feelings, beliefs, or values could be at play?

Find out how to deal with these possible problems or conflicts. How will you talk to each other, negotiate, or find a middle ground? What rules or agreements need to be made in order to build trust and respect?

Think about what these potential problems could mean for your relationship as a whole. How will they change your shared values, how you talk to each other, or how you connect? How will you both grow, learn, and change?

For Long-term Relationships:

It's important to keep the lines of communication open as relationships grow and interests change. Talking about each other's hobbies and how you feel about them can help you continue to understand, accept, and find a middle ground.

EPILOGUE

As we come to the end of this exploration of the many different parts of relationships, we realize that love, in all its beauty and complexity, is not a place but a journey. The goal of this book was to give you the tools, insights, and guiding questions you need to help you and your partner talk to each other, feel empathy for each other, and understand each other better. From the silly to the deep, the topics explored show how emotions, beliefs, fears, and wants are woven together to make up the human connection.

Relationships are not fixed things, but rather things that grow, change, and sometimes even test us in ways we didn't expect. The questions and advice were meant to help you and your partner build a connection that is more honest, understanding, and strong. Whether you're just starting a new relationship or trying to keep a long-term one going, there are always new things to learn.

Remember that there is no one right way to love and be in a relationship. What makes your relationship special is the fact that you are both different and that you have had similar experiences. It is also important that you respect and understand each other. Accept the uncertainty, admit the flaws, and be happy about the growth.

May you find joy and laughter in the easy times and strength and resiliency when things get tough. As you continue to explore, learn, and grow with your partner, remember that love is not just about finding the right person, but also about making the right relationship.

May this book be a trusted friend on your journey and a gentle reminder that the path of love, even if it's sometimes winding and unknown, is full of opportunities to learn, grow, and find happiness.

Here's to your own journey, the dreams you share, your own growth, and most of all, your loving and thriving relationship. May the questions bring you joy, the answers bring you wisdom, and every step you take together bring you love.

PLEASE CONSIDER LEAVING A REVIEW

Hello there!

As an author, I know just how important reviews are for getting the word out about my work. When readers leave a review on Amazon or any other book stores, it helps others discover my book and decide whether it's right for them.

Plus, it gives me valuable feedback on what readers enjoyed and what they didn't.

So if you've read my book and enjoyed it (or even if you didn't!), I would really appreciate it if you took a moment to leave a review on Amazon. It doesn't have to be long or complicated - just a few words about what you thought of the book would be incredibly helpful.

Thank you so much for your support!

Jeff

ALSO BY JEFFREY C. CHAMPAN

Adulting Hard for Young Men

• • • ● • ● • • •

Adulting Hard for Young Women

Adulting Hard After College

Adulting Hard in Your Late Twenties and Thirties

Adulting Hard For Couples

• • • ● • ● • • •

Adulting Hard for New Parents

• • • ● • ● • • •

Printed in Great Britain
by Amazon

37717410R00208